新综合
大学英语

INTEGRATED COLLEGE ENGLISH

3

学生用书
Student's Book

总 主 编　　庄智象

主　　编　　张　健　　王跃武

编　　者　　赵美娟　　史志康
　　　　　　王雪梅　　常　辉

清华大学出版社
北　京

版权所有，侵权必究。举报：010-62782989，beiqinquan@tup.tsinghua.edu.cn。

图书在版编目（CIP）数据

新综合大学英语学生用书. 3 / 庄智象总主编；张健，王跃武主编. —北京：清华大学出版社，2022.6
ISBN 978-7-302-60808-0

Ⅰ. ①新… Ⅱ. ①庄… ②张… ③王… Ⅲ. ①英语-高等学校-教学 Ⅳ. ①H319.39

中国版本图书馆 CIP 数据核字（2022）第 080007 号

策划编辑：郝建华
责任编辑：刘　艳
封面设计：子　一
责任校对：王凤芝
责任印制：丛怀宇

出版发行：清华大学出版社
　　　网　　址：http://www.tup.com.cn，http://www.wqbook.com
　　　地　　址：北京清华大学学研大厦 A 座　　邮　编：100084
　　　社 总 机：010-83470000　　　　　　　　邮　购：010-62786544
　　　投稿与读者服务：010-62776969，c-service@tup.tsinghua.edu.cn
　　　质 量 反 馈：010-62772015，zhiliang@tup.tsinghua.edu.cn
印 装 者：北京盛通印刷股份有限公司
经　　销：全国新华书店
开　　本：210mm×285mm　　印　张：16　　字　数：387 千字
版　　次：2022 年 7 月第 1 版　　　　　　印　次：2022 年 7 月第 1 次印刷
定　　价：78.00 元

产品编号：084159-01

总 序

中国特色社会主义进入新时代，我国全面建成小康社会，实现了第一个百年奋斗目标，又乘势而上开启了全面建设社会主义现代化国家的新征程，向第二个百年奋斗目标进军。在这极其关键的中华民族伟大复兴的征程中，无论是文化交融、文明互鉴，经济全球化发展，"一带一路"建设，人类命运共同体构建，还是国家高质量发展，世界一流高校和学科建设，都需要我国的高等教育担负起历史的重任，为国家、为民族、为人类的进步事业培养和造就千百万具有家国情怀和全球视野，了解国际事务治理，精通专业，掌握外语，胜任国际合作，具有参与国际竞争能力的高素质、创新型人才。在这新征程中，国家各项事业的发展对高质量高等教育的需要，对科学知识和优秀人才的需求，比以往任何时候都更为迫切！有鉴于此，我们策划、组织编写了"新综合大学英语系列教材"。

教育部颁布的《普通高等学校教材管理办法》指出："双一流"高校与高水平大学应发挥学科优势，组织编写教材，提升我国教材的原创性，打造精品教材。教材的质量和水准直接关系到人才培养目标的实现，对人才培养起着至关重要的作用。教材建设要关注科技发展动态和经济社会发展趋势，着眼未来，着眼创新人才和技术技能复合型人才培养需要。"新综合大学英语系列教材"的研发编写团队，认真研读国家对教材编写提出的新要求，领会其精神实质，充分领悟"教材体现国家意志，其核心功能是育人"的重要性，始终坚持正确的政治方向，牢固树立正确的世界观、人生观和价值观，大力弘扬社会主义核心价值观，倡导健康、积极向上的精神，充分贯彻并体现"为党育人、为国育才"的理念和责任。"新综合大学英语系列教材"贯彻国家高等教育高质量发展人才培养目标要求，依据教育部《大学英语教学指南》（2020版）及相关文件精神，对大学英语教学现状、需求和未来发展趋势进行大量调查分析的基础上研发编写而成，既能满足当下人才培养之需求，又极具前瞻性。

"新综合大学英语系列教材"重视和倡导语言能力综合发展，强调和突出就同一主题融合听、说、读、写、译能力的训练和发展，打破按技能分册编写、教师分课型教学的模式，力求语言、知识、文化、技能学习和训练深度融合，帮助学生实现综合能力和素质有效提升至新的高度。其主要特色是：

1 培根铸魂、启智润心，全面落实立德树人的根本任务

"新综合大学英语系列教材"在研发编写中，以全面贯彻党的教育方针、落实立德树人的任务为根本，全程贯彻课程思政。从教材的整体设计、理念确定、框架构建、素材遴选、内容与形式抉择、练习设计与编写、问题设置与讨论、资源配置与使用等各个方面，努力传递正能量，激励学生奋发向上，积极进取；引导学生增强"四个意识"，坚定"四个自信"，做到"两个维护"，践行社会主义核心价值观；帮助学生树立正确的世界观、人生观和价值观，努力成为既有家国情怀，又有国际视野和全球胜任力的中国特色社会主义建设者和接班人。

2 融合语言、知识、文化、技能学习和训练，着重发展综合能力

"新综合大学英语系列教材"在大量调查研究的基础上，研判学科复合、学科交叉、学科跨界、学科融合发展趋势，充分意识到这是学科、专业高水平发展的必由之路。无论是学科知识、语言知识、文化知识，还是语言技能的学习和发展，都日趋复合、综合，渐入融合之势不可避免。同时，随着教育体系的建设和发展，制度的不断完善，教育教学更加系统、全面、完整，从学龄前教育教学到高等教育教学，重视全人（the whole person）教育成为必然的发展模式。强化和补缺式的单项技能或能力的培养需求逐渐弱化或减少，割裂式外语教学、单项技能的教学和训练将不断变弱、淡出，而就同一题材从多方面进行领会和产出的综合训练日趋受到青睐。"新综合大学英语系列教材"审时度势，力求外语教育教学厚实基础、广博知识、综合发展和提升语言能力。词汇、语法、听说读写译深度融合，各项技能训练、能力培养融为一体，各就其位，各司其职，相互观照，彼此促进，科学复现，有机循环，融会贯通，达到高效的教学效果。

3 融通中外，促进文化交融、文明互鉴

无论是经济全球化发展、"一带一路"建设、人类命运共同体构建，还是高质量发展的追求，都要求中国更多地了解世界，让世界更多地了解中国，增强中西文化交流和中外融通。"新综合大学英语系列教材"无论是课文前名言警句的选用，还是语篇和其他素材的遴选，包括练习的设计，都力求做到既展现目标语民族的文化与文明，又推介中华文化与文明，尤其是今日中华之新貌，努力讲好中国故事，传播好中国声音，提升学生的国际交流和沟通能力，为融通中外，促进文化交融、文明互鉴做出积极努力和贡献。

4 展现时代特点，主题丰富、内容完整，提质增效

"新综合大学英语系列教材"按主题单元设计，循培根铸魂、启智增慧标准选择语篇和其他素材，依语言认知、学习规律设计活动，编写练习。力求题材丰富、体裁多样，内容、信息贴近学习、生活和社会，反映当下，展望未来，引导学生积极向上，奋发进取。语篇既有宏大叙事，又有微观描述；既探讨哲理、学识、人生，又论及自然、人类、社会发展；既关注个人学业和职业发展，又心系社会、国家和人类进步。力求主题、内容、形式完美匹配；语言、知识、文化相互关照；技能、能力、素质融合发展，切实有助于完善学生的知识结构，力求提质增效。

5 力求"教有实效、学有实效"，促进教育教学高质量发展

"新综合大学英语系列教材"的语篇和素材遴选，力求语言真实地道，内容新颖，兼具思想性、知识性、科学性、人文性、时代性和趣味性等，能激发学生求知欲和学习兴趣。词汇、语法、视听说、阅读、写作、翻译教学活动设计和练习编写，力求内涵丰富，形式新颖，语言真实，文化多元，生动有趣，特色鲜明，科学完美。着力培养学生的语言应用能力，培育语感，传授正确的学习方法。词语模块以预构成语块（prefab）（即常用句套子、词语搭配、动词用法

结构等）为主体开展学习和练习，以确保学生交际时使用的语言地道、得体，并提高其理解能力和表达的流利程度。语法技能（grammaring）模块力图通过操练，将语法知识转化成语法运用技能，以提升学生语言理解力和表达的准确性。翻译模块通过两种语言的对译和比较，增强学生的语言意识（language awareness），使其领悟语言学习的正确方法。视听说、写作模块通过仿说和仿写形式进行产出练习，提供示范对话和语篇，让学生以相应的语言形式和内容信息进行说能和写能训练，习得用地道、得体的语言进行流利表达的能力，促进教育教学高质量发展。

6 创新教学理念、方法和手段，提升能级

"新综合大学英语系列教材"力求在编写理念、指导原则和教学法思想等方面有所创新，既继承和弘扬中国大学外语教育教学的长处、成功经验和特色，又积极吸收和借鉴海外新鲜、先进、有益的经验和成果，扬长避短，兼收并蓄，探索融合教学，努力探寻合乎中国大学英语教学需要和特色的教学理念、方法、手段和模式。"新综合大学英语系列教材"重视教学内容、形式、方法融入现代技术，充分开发和利用数字平台、数字资源以及能有效提高教学质量与水平的教学资源，实体虚拟、线下线上、静态动态、自然智能、人工智能，多模态互动，提升教学能级。

"新综合大学英语系列教材"创新编写模式，采用纵向打通、模块分工负责制：第1至第4册的课文前名言警句由王雪梅教授选定、史志康教授翻译和评论；词汇部分由常辉教授团队编写；阅读部分由王雪梅教授团队编写；翻译部分由张健教授编写；语法技能部分由赵美娟教授编写；视听说部分由王跃武教授团队编写；写作部分由史志康教授编写。教材各册实行主编负责制：常辉、王雪梅主编第1册；王雪梅、常辉主编第2册；张健、王跃武主编第3册；王跃武、张健主编第4册。杨惠中教授担任顾问、庄智象教授担任总主编，负责教材的总体策划和设计：编写理念、原则的确定，框架建构，编写工作的组织和协调，内容审查和质量控制等。

"新综合大学英语系列教材"的出版发行，是编写团队历经数年的学习、探索、实践、研讨，通力合作、辛勤付出的成果，是集体汗水和智慧的结晶。编写团队全体成员为此牺牲了很多个人爱好和兴趣，克服了诸多困难，付出了许多辛劳。谨向他们致以深深的敬意，并表示衷心的感谢！祁寿华教授对教材进行了仔细的审校，谨向他致以诚挚的谢意！上海时代教育出版研究中心参与了教材的研发并给予各方面的支持；清华大学出版社的领导对教材的编写和出版给予了大力的支持和帮助，编辑团队精心编审，严格把关，保证了教材的出版质量和出版进度，谨在此一并致谢。

限于水平和时间，教材难免存在不尽如人意之处，舛误恐难免，恳请老师和同学们批评指正，以期不断完善！

杨惠中　庄智象
2022年5月

编者的话

新时代，为贯彻新发展理念，各级各类学校要全面贯彻党的教育方针，落实立德树人根本任务；为党育人，为国育才；培养德、智、体、美、劳全面发展的社会主义建设者和接班人。教育部制定的《大学英语教学指南》（2020版）明确提出了大学英语课程思政的要求。"新综合大学英语系列教材"正是落实上述指导思想，对照大学英语课程培养目标和要求，在广泛调查分析大学英语教学现状和研判未来发展趋势的基础上，遵循外语学习规律，精心策划和组织编写而成。

一、编写理念

本系列教材对接大学英语教学要求，注重培养学生的英语应用能力、思辨能力和人文精神，增强跨文化交际意识和能力，发展自主学习能力，突出科学性、综合性、导向性和个性化，重视预构成语块学习、语法技能操练、浸入式教学，在课文遴选、板块设计、练习编写等方面守正创新，突出特色。

1 科学选材

本系列教材中教学素材的选择科学全面。首先，充分考虑了内容的思想性和语言的规范性，注重时代性、知识性、新颖性、趣味性、文化性、可教性等，既重视课文的经典性，又重视内容的人文性。其次，选材多样而真实，既有文学作品，又有科学小品文；既有经典寓言，又有名篇演讲，原汁原味，最大程度地保留原文的真实性。再次，课文在文章长度、词汇量、难易度等方面根据能力等级加以科学控制，做到由易到难，循序渐进；Text B 作为补充阅读材料，文章的主题与 Text A 匹配，难度略低于 Text A，字数略多于 Text A。此外，考虑到"相同的材料，听懂难于读懂"这一外语学习的普遍规律，听力材料的难度比 Text A 略低。

2 分级、有效教学

遵循"有效教学"的编写指导思想，力求做到"教有实效、学有实效"。教材编写不针对学校类型分层，而是从学生的实际英语起点水平、能力等级要求出发，分阶段设计，以便各校根据自身实际情况安排教学，选择和使用教材。

3 综合性语言技能培养

不同于传统大学英语教材视听说和读写译教学割裂开来的现状，本系列教材融视听说和读写译于一体，强调听、说、读、写、译能力的综合培养，内容围绕同一主题展开，体现融合特色，突破不同语言技能割裂式教学的局限性。

4　导向式语言学习策略运用

围绕不同话题与情景进行操练，强调"做中学"，同时提供相应听、说、读、写、译等策略，不仅有助于培养学生的语言应用能力，而且有助于提升其语言学习策略的运用能力。

5　预构成语块有效习得

英语中的单词不是孤立地使用的，通常跟搭配、词语用法等形成固定结构，被称为"预构成语块"（prefab）。英语学习过程中必须把预构成语块当作一个单位，如同一个单词一样来操练和记忆。重视预构成语块的教学不但可以帮助学生有效培育语感，提升英语表达的地道性和流利性，而且能帮助学生掌握正确学习英语的方法，使其终身受益。在教材编写过程中，充分运用语料库，通过真实例句与练习，科学选择并指导学生有效学习预构成语块。

6　语法技能操练

学习语言的目的是形成正确使用语言的技能，而不仅仅是为了掌握语言知识。本系列教材高度重视语法技能操练（grammaring），采用"习惯养成技巧"（habit-forming technique），帮助学生掌握语法学习的重点和要点，扎扎实实地习得语法技能。语法技能操练形式活泼，融枯燥的语法知识于多样化的练习中，通过语法点在听、说、读、写、译等不同练习中的复现，使学生有效掌握语法要点和相关句型的交际功能，切实提升语言交际能力。

7　浸入式课程思政

重视培养学生的创新思辨能力、家国情怀和国际视野。所选课文主题具有哲理性和思辨意义，所提供的众多名言警句不仅传播中华优秀文化，更强调社会主义核心价值观的培育。语法、翻译、阅读、写作、视听说等相关练习均有效融入育人理念和典型的思政元素，实现"春风化雨，润物无声"的思政育人效果，达到立德树人目标。

二、教材结构

本系列教材共 4 册，每册含 8 个单元，每个单元主要由 Text A 和 Text B 及配套练习构成。Text A 为每个单元的主要部分，由词汇、阅读、语法、翻译、视听说、写作等任务构成，从不同维度培养学生的语言运用能力。Initial Reading 和 Study Reading 聚焦阅读训练，Word Building 和 Grammaring 侧重词汇、翻译和语法学习，Communicating 强调视听、说、写，注重跨文化交际能力培养。Text B 是 Text A 的延伸，选取主题相近的文章精心编写相应练习，以进一步扩展学生的词汇量并提升其阅读和翻译等能力。每个单元的结构如下：

Text A	
Warming Up	Quotations
Initial Reading	Vocabulary
	Skimming
Notes	
Study Reading	Structure Analysis
	Reading Comprehension
Word Building	Blank Filling: Active Words
	Prefab Translation
	Partial Dictation
	Sentence Translation
	Translation Tips
Grammaring	Explanation
	Practice
Communicating	Viewing
	Speaking
	Writing

Text B	
Notes	
Reading for Gist	
Reading for Details	
Reading Beyond	
Prefabs	
Sentence Translation	

三、使用建议

1 课时分配

建议每个单元基本按照 8 个课时安排教学，可根据内容难度、学校课时及学生实际英语水平适当调整。具体分配如下：

第 1、第 2 课时：Text A 的导入。就 Text A 的作者、写作背景、文章大意等进行讲解与讨论，并完成 Warming Up 和 Initial Reading 两个板块以及 Study Reading 中的 Structure Analysis 部分的练习。

第 3、第 4 课时：Text A 的篇章理解。讲解文中重点词汇及语法点，并深入分析篇章布局，引导学生把握语篇的主旨要义，同时，完成 Study Reading 中 Reading Comprehension 部分的练习和 Word Building、Grammaring 练习。

第 5、第 6 课时：Text A 的视听说写部分。完成整个 Communicating 板块。

第 7、第 8 课时：Text B。理解 Text B 文章并选择完成相应的练习及活动；回答学生对该单元的有关提问，进行答疑辅导。

2 内容安排与教学建议

Text A

Warming Up

名言警句均与单元主题相关，且多选自经典作品或名家论述，具有哲理价值或现实意义，辅以文笔优雅、意味隽永的评述。教师在授课时，可要求学生在对名言警句进行翻译的基础上展开深入讨论，激活其认知图式，引导他们切入单元主题，深入思考并形成自己的判断与观点，以培养创新思辨能力和口头表达能力。

Initial Reading

1) Vocabulary

选择课文中的难词，一般在 20 个左右，旨在辅助初读，减少阅读困难，同时培养学生阅读时猜测词义的能力。

2) Skimming

要求学生在规定时间内（视文章长短、难易度和学生的实际英语水平而定）读完全文，掌握文章大意。学生需根据对篇章的理解，从所给定的 10 个与课文内容相关的陈述句中选择符合主旨大意或细节的句子。该部分旨在培养学生的快速略读能力。教师授课时可要求学生进行个人快速阅读练习或者小组竞赛。

Notes

该部分选取 Text A 中涉及的专有名词、修辞手法、文化知识、难句、语法点等进行注释，旨在帮助学生加深对课文的理解，增强人文素养，拓展跨文化知识。教师可引导学生在预习课文时参考，并运用相关知识理解课文。

Study Reading

1) Structure Analysis

主要讨论课文的篇章结构，考查并培养学生对宏观语篇结构的分析能力，提高学生的语篇意识。学生需在理解重要和关键细节的基础上，掌握作者行文的内在逻辑，简要概括段落要点。同时，该题型也与其他部分的内容相呼应，强化学生对重点词汇和短语的学习。

2) Reading Comprehension

Sequencing：该部分为句子排序题，选用课文中不同段落的句子，借助释义等方式变换句子的表达方式，要求学生基于句义判断该句所在段落，进而根据句子位置进行排序。该题旨在帮助学生借助关键信息进行意义判断与句子定位，培养学生的语言知识应用与语篇分析能力。

Blank Filling：以句子填空的形式考查学生对重点词汇的理解及表达能力。所考查的知识点源于课文中的单词、常用短语或预构成语块，要求学生从课文中选词填写，并在填写时注意形式的变化。该题的语言表达基于课文，重点考查学生对预构成语块的理解及其在不同语境下的运用。教师讲授课文后，可要求学生课下自主完成该练习，课上检查提问或进行拓展式讲解。

Group Work：该部分属于迁移创新类练习，要求学生围绕课文主题，针对某一观点或者话题，进行小组讨论并展示汇报。该题旨在培养学生的思辨能力、团队协作与沟通交流能力。教师可结合课文内容，对小组讨论的维度与方式进行指导，可要求学生在课堂上讨论并汇报，或课后研讨、课上汇报，或将相关汇报的 PPT 上传到线上教学平台进行展示交流。

Word Building

1) Prefabs

Blank Filling: Active Words：选择课文中的常用重点动词或形容词，数量一般为 12 个左右，先给出释义、常见搭配和用法，再从语料库选取真实语料设计与该词相关的搭配练习，培养学生的词汇搭配能力和意识。教师在授课时可先让学生学习这些词汇，再给予一定时间让学生完成练习，并进行拓展。

Prefab Translation：侧重培养学生语义语用、语境语感以及惯用搭配等方面的语言意识，引导学生熟悉重要词语或词组的用法；围绕相关语言要点，采用汉译英的练习形式对学生进行考查，使其在日后的翻译实践中能够举一反三，触类旁通。教师在授课时可让学生先讨论预构成语块的汉语释义，再让他们完成翻译练习。

2) Partial Dictation

以听写填空的形式考查学生的听力技能和重点词汇及表达形式的掌握程度，要求学生在理解课文、掌握积极词汇和预构成语块的基础上，以听力练习的形式完成 8 个句子。每句要求填 3~5 个词。教师可在讲解课文后，将此作为课后作业让学生自主完成。

3) Sentence Translation

选取若干常用词语或词组考查学生对它们的运用能力，帮助学生通过笔译实践逐步培养翻译技能，提高翻译能力。教师可分两次在课堂上要求学生进行笔译实践并加以讲解点评，建议按教材中练习的编排顺序和难易程度展开。若教学课时不足，建议教师选择部分或全部作为学生的课后作业，用以提高和检测学生英汉互译的综合能力。

4) Translation Tips

以较为轻松的漫谈形式讲解翻译原理和技巧，引导并提高学生发现问题、分析问题和解决问题的能力，提升语言意识，理解英汉两种语言的差异。所阐释的翻译原理和技巧主要是提示性的，突出重点，解决难点，力求言简意赅，深入浅出，明白易懂；所举典型译例也是示范性的，贴近现实生活，便于教师举一反三，丰富讲课内容。

Grammaring

语法技能操练部分围绕课文中的典型语言点，帮助学生理解语法形式及其表达的意义和交际功能，以便正确掌握语法形式在具体语境中的用法，学会在特定语境中灵活运用恰当的语法形式。

每单元重点学习 2~3 个语法点。语法点选自 Text A 中的典型语法结构，每个语法点下设语法讲解和语法练习两部分。语法讲解旨在让学生了解语法形式的特点及其意义和用法。语法练习旨在通过针对性的练习使学生不仅掌握语法知识，且将语法知识运用到具体语境中，提高语言应用的准确性。

授课时，教师对语法规则的讲解应简明扼要，采用启发式教学，让学生自主归纳和发现语法规律。语法练习可采用边练边讲的方式，也可采用同伴互评等方式，重点分析中国学习者语法学习的难点和要点，并结合使用场景和语境进行操练。

Communicating

1) Viewing

旨在培养学生的英语视听能力，提高他们听懂与本单元主题相关的真实英语视听材料的能力，主要训练四项听力技能，分如下步骤进行：

Get Prepared：介绍与视频内容相关的背景信息、专有名词、生词及预构成语块，以降低听力理解的难度，帮助学生在视听过程中重构意义。练习内容和形式有理解图片、回答问题、短文填空、朗读等。教师可要求学生课前完成此练习，课堂上检查，开放式问题可采用讨论形式。

Watch and Listen for Gist：训练学生理解视频材料主旨大意的能力。练习采用回答问题、选择、填空等形式。教师可要求听力能力较弱的同学课前预听。授课时，重点考查学生听懂主旨大意的能力，必要时教师可重复播放视频，确保绝大部分同学听懂大意。

Watch and Listen for Details：帮助学生理解视频材料的重要信息或细节。题型包括选择、填空、回答问题、正误判断等。授课时，教师可提示学生先看题目，以便观看视频时有的放矢，将注意力聚焦于相关信息。

Watch and Listen for Implied Meaning / Watch and Infer Information：帮助学生理解说话人的态度、言外之意、真实意图，或根据视频推断其中隐含的意义或信息。题型为回答问题、填充答案等。授课时，教师需注意引导和启发。根据视频材料的具体情况，第四、五、八单元未设此练习。

Watch and Listen for Language Use：培养学生的语言意识，做到脚踏实地，不仅能听得懂，还写得出，活学活用。练习题型为听写，要求学生写出短句、预构成语块、关键词等。授课时，教师还可根据学生的实际水平，增加多样练习形式，如要求学生翻译、跟读、配音（放视频时隐去原声，学生大声说英语）、上台表演等，做到真正学懂、会用。根据视频材料的具体情况，第六单元未设此练习。

2) Speaking

旨在训练学生开口说英语的能力，包含两个活动，练习形式包括仿说、个人发言、分组讨论、上台演讲、角色表演等。

Activity 1

示范对话或演讲：训练学生听懂并学习示范对话或演讲。授课时，教师可先要求学生不看文本，只听录音，听懂对话或演讲后再看文本，然后重新播放音频，让学生听音填空（主要是预构成语块）。

配对练习：训练学生熟练掌握以上示范对话或演讲。教师可要求学生配对操练，至少轮换角色朗读两遍以上，尽量做到不看文本能够进行对话或演讲。

交际功能与表达手段：介绍与本单元相关的交际功能及与之对应的语言表达手段（教材中用斜体标识）。教师可要求学生跟读、复读，直至熟练掌握。

配对仿说：训练学生在掌握示范对话、相关交际功能和语言表达手段之后，能够利用给出的相关图表或其他信息，配对或分组讨论本单元的相关话题。教师授课时应注意因材施教：英语基础较弱的学生可只做仿说练习，不做自由讨论或发言。

Activity 2

问题导入：以提问、图表、问卷等形式导入讨论的话题和信息，激发学生的参与热情和更多思考，便于学生讨论和发表意见。

自由讨论：训练学生学会就本单元话题开展自由讨论，发表个人意见。练习形式为小组讨论、个人发言等，并提供示范对话。在课堂教学中，教师应鼓励所有学生积极参与口语活动；可根据授课班级的实际情况，组织学生进行小组讨论，鼓励或邀请学生上台发言或进行角色表演。本项课堂活动语言难度较高，教师可根据学生的实际水平确定如何展开。

3) Writing

包括短文填空和短文写作两个练习，旨在训练学生学以致用，把本单元学到的重要英语短语和词汇运用到书面表达中。短文填空旨在复习本单元中出现的重点语言表达，主要是预构成语块。教师可要求学生课前做好练习，课堂上提问、核对答案和讲解。短文写作要求学生在掌握相应的语言表达后，独立写一篇长度约为 220 词、题材与课文内容相关的短文。教师可让学生课后自主完成作文并进行同伴互评。在课堂上，教师可以对学生的作文进行选择性或总结性的讲评。

Text B

Text B 充分考虑学生的兴趣和水平，选取体裁丰富、题材多样的文本，并与 Text A 主题一致。此部分辅以生词旁注、课文注释，并设计了段落匹配、判断正误、问答或者开放式讨论、词汇练习、中英互译等形式的练习，旨在帮助学生加深对课文的理解，提升其信息处理能力、语言鉴赏能力、跨文化交际能力和思辨能力等。具体练习形式因篇章不同而有所变化。

Notes

该部分选取 Text B 中出现的人名、地名、历史事件等文化点进行注释，帮助学生减少阅读障碍，丰富跨文化知识，拓展视野。教师可鼓励学生讨论部分注释，在课上或课下分享观点。

Reading for Gist

主要通过问答题的形式，考查学生对课文的理解。问答题基于 Text B 的课文内容设置开放式问题，要求学生在理解课文大意的基础上，讨论文中相关观点。教师授课时可将学生分成小组，围绕所涉及的话题或观点进行讨论或辩论，然后让学生以小组汇报形式呈现讨论结果，教师予以点评。教师可将该题用于课文预习或者复习阶段，既可作为课前速读练习，也可作为课后作业要求学生自主完成。

Reading for Details

一般为段落匹配题或者句子判断题。要求学生根据每题的表述内容，将其匹配到相应段落，或者描述每段的主题，主要考查学生概括归纳段落大意、提取重要信息的能力，以加深对课文的理解。句子判断题要求学生根据课文内容判断句子正误，主要训练学生的略读、寻读等阅读技能，提升学生归纳总结、逻辑关联、预测和同义转换等能力。教师可在课上布置学生完成并抽检，或者借助线上教学平台检查完成情况。

Reading Beyond

一般为开放式的小组讨论题或问答题，旨在考查学生对课文结构与内容的理解，促进预构成语块的使用与内化，提升学生的逻辑思维能力与表达能力，并培养其核心价值观和人文素养。小组讨论题要求学生就文中观点、社会现象等展开讨论或探究，并分享自己的观点。问答题要求学生对课文中的重要内容，如关键信息或较有哲理的句子，进行推理讨论。教师可要求学生课后分组完成，在线上教学平台上分享小组观点，或者在课上进行小组汇报；也可要求学生结合讨论完成相应的写作任务。

Prefabs

选取 Text B 中出现的常用预构成语块，要求学生在阅读后写出汉语，旨在加强学生的预构成语块意识，使他们掌握地道的英语表达方式，培养英语语感。教师可让学生阅读课文时猜测这些预构成语块在文中的意思，并用汉语写出来；教师分析课文时，可帮助学生理解这些预构成语块在文中的意思，并进行适当的拓展。

Sentence Translation

包括英译汉和汉译英两个题型，主要考查学生对预构成语块和句型的理解，以及适切的英汉语书面表达能力。英译汉选取课文中重要的或者较难理解的句子，要求学生译为汉语。汉译英选取重要的预构成语块，要求学生将其用到句子翻译中。教师可将该部分作为课后练习，要求学生完成并上传到线上教学平台或者微信群进行小组互评。

本教材词汇部分由常辉教授团队编写，阅读部分由王雪梅教授团队编写，翻译部分由张健教授编写，语法技能部分由赵美娟教授编写，视听说部分由王跃武教授团队编写，写作部分由史志康教授编写。此外，胡萌萌、纪小凌、宋开颜、王栋、赵勇、周岸勤参与了词汇部分的编写，姜霞、亓明俊、孙钦美、徐启豪、赵双花、朱神海参与了阅读部分的编写，高宇鑫和蒋超群参与了第三册教师用书中部分课文译文的编写，马韬和宋艳参与了视听说部分的编写，在此表示感谢。囿于编写团队水平，书中疏漏在所难免，敬请广大读者批评指正。

编　者

2022 年 5 月

Contents

Unit	Reading	Vocabulary	Translation
UNIT 1 Ignorance Page 1	**Text A** Page 3 The Pleasures of Ignorance **Text B** Page 24 Viewing Nature's Beauty Through a New Lens **About Reading:** Using Fix-up Strategies	**Active Words:** ignorance, miserable, sufficient, ignorant, descend, absurd, enthusiasm, conquer, confirm, assure, confine, fame	**Translation Tips:** From a Bird's Song to Animal Voices
UNIT 2 Communication Page 31	**Text A** Page 33 How to Become an Effective Communicator in a Business Context **Text B** Page 53 The Long-term Career Damage from Not Talking to Your Kids About Money **About Reading:** Questioning	**Active Words:** context, contribute, innovative, proposal, conflict, interact, image, factor, mutual, essential, establish, specific	**Translation Tips:** Vivid Words, Big Thrills
UNIT 3 Volunteering Page 59	**Text A** Page 61 The Value of Volunteering **Text B** Page 83 How to Find the Right Volunteer Opportunity **About Reading:** Determining Main Ideas	**Active Words:** commitment, recruit, individual, community, acquire, expand, contact, promote, current, ignore, dynamic, undermine, diverse, distort	**Translation Tips:** "Hospice" and Its Corresponding Expressions in Chinese
UNIT 4 Innovation Page 89	**Text A** Page 91 Yesterday's Country: Not to Worry, They Can't Innovate **Text B** Page 113 The Functions of WeChat **About Reading:** Using Sensory Images	**Active Words:** innovate, maintain, shrink, confidence, deteriorate, military, suicide, response, prohibit, threaten, crucial, rely, erect, extend	**Translation Tips:** Dynamic Equivalents for "Making China Great Again"

Grammaring*	Viewing	Speaking	Writing
may/might, could, must + perfect infinitive prepositions in relative clauses genitive -'s	**Video:** Happy Elephants	**Activity 1:** Can Animals Think like Humans Do? **Activity 2:** How Much Do You Know About the Human Brain?	Views on Ignorance and Knowledge
introducing examples: *for example, such as…* sentence connectors: *however, therefore*	**Video:** Business Communication	**Activity 1:** Body Language **Activity 2:** How to Be an Active Listener?	Views on Business Communication
articles: *a, an, the* sentence connectors: listing (*first, second, …*) prepositions: *for, of, to*	**Video:** Volunteering for Something	**Activity 1:** Why Do I Want to Do Volunteer Work? **Activity 2:** I Want to Volunteer for…	Views on the Value of Volunteering
subject-verb concord prepositions: *from, on, with* adjectives ending in *-ing* or *-ed*	**Video:** China's 5G Network	**Activity 1:** What Electronic Media Do You Like? **Activity 2:** What Is 5G?	Views on Chinese Dream

* 该板块各级标题形式多样，故未采用实词首字母大写原则。

Contents

Unit	Reading	Vocabulary	Translation
UNIT 5 Passion Page 119	**Text A** Page 121 Delicacy of Taste and Delicacy of Passion **Text B** Page 142 A New Sensation: Recording and Reproducing Taste **About Reading:** Vocabulary-building Strategy	**Active Words:** passion, grief, provoke, distinction, contempt, disposition, deprive, resemble, prosperity, perceive, disgust, remedy, endeavour, render, external	**Translation Tips:** "Not to Mention" and Its Near Expressions
UNIT 6 Language Learning Page 149	**Text A** Page 151 Why Is the Native Language Learnt So Well? **Text B** Page 172 Embracing the Ambiguity **About Reading:** Activating or Building Background Knowledge	**Active Words:** comparison, visual, flexible, acquire, detect, favorable, attempt, fulfill, awkward, sympathy, accuracy	**Translation Tips:** Translating "Organ Words" Properly
UNIT 7 Reading Page 179	**Text A** Page 181 How to Read **Text B** Page 200 Sweet Potato Porridge **About Reading:** Previewing	**Active Words:** enforce, prejudice, acquaint, definite, element, distinct, tragic, vision, reveal, reflection, destiny, perspective, confuse, perception	**Translation Tips:** From "Fellow-Worker" to "Migrant Worker" and the Like
UNIT 8 Generosity Page 207	**Text A** Page 209 True Generosity Involves More than Just Giving **Text B** Page 230 Why We Should Always Be Kind to Strangers **About Reading:** Predictions and Inferences	**Active Words:** complicated, qualify, generous, consistent, propose, controversial, incline, attach, charity, illustrate, compatible	**Translation Tips:** The Word "Matter" Matters a Lot

Grammaring	Viewing	Speaking	Writing
existential *there* *as… as*: comparing equal amounts	**Video:** Audrey Hepburn	**Activity 1:** What Are You Talking About? **Activity 2:** Unwelcome Questions	Views on Taste and Passion
however + adj./adv. plural-only nouns	**Video:** Babies' Acquisition of Language	**Activity 1:** Do You Like Learning Languages? **Activity 2:** Child Language Development and More	Views on Language Learning
as: with special word order to express concession directive + *and/or…*	**Video:** Old Reading Habits	**Activity 1:** Reading Is Important. **Activity 2:** How Much Do You Read?	Views on How to Read
past perfect Type 3 conditional	**Video:** Extraordinary Altruists	**Activity 1:** Let's Talk About Compassion. **Activity 2:** What Will You Do with Things You Do Not Need Anymore?	Views on Generosity

Unit 1 Ignorance

Warming Up

Memorize and comment on the following quotations on ignorance.

1 知之为知之，不知为不知，是知也。

——孔子

2 Ignorance is preferable to error, and he is less remote from the truth who believes nothing than he who believes what is wrong.

— Thomas Jefferson

INITIAL READING

A Vocabulary

Read the new words aloud and try to work out their meanings in the text.

New Words

5	**beech** /biːtʃ/ n.		18	**quiver** /ˈkwɪvə(r)/ vi.
6	**elm** /elm/ n.		19	**avenge** /əˈvendʒ/ vt.
6	**thrush** /θrʌʃ/ n.		19	**lurk** /lɜːk/ vi.
6	**blackbird** /ˈblækbɜːd/ n.		20	**naturalist** /ˈnætʃrəlɪst/ n.
10	**feeble** /ˈfiːbl/ adj.		21	**sober** /ˈsəʊbə(r)/ adj.
11	**chaffinch** /ˈtʃæfɪntʃ/ n.		22	**plodding** /ˈplɒdɪŋ/ adj.
11	**cuckoo** /ˈkʊkuː/ n.		30	**dabble** /ˈdæbl/ vi.
14	**dew** /djuː/ n.		36	**dogma** /ˈdɒgmə/ n.
16	**spectacle** /ˈspektəkl/ n.		36	**stiffen** /ˈstɪfn/ vi.
18	**halt** /hɔːlt/ vi.		37	**omniscient** /ɒmˈnɪsiənt/ adj.

B Skimming

Read Text A and go through the statements within eight minutes. Circle the numbers of the correct statements.

1　People become educated when they realize that they are ignorant.

2　The main idea of this essay is the significance of not being knowledgeable.

3　Urban dwellers are unexceptionally astonished by the stretched land they see while strolling along the countryside.

4　Barely can the difference of the chirping of birds be discernible because birds sing in a similar voice.

5　Everything has its advantages and disadvantages. So does ignorance.

6　Ignorance, on the bright side, brings people elevated joy through a sense of originality.

7　To gain the unseen treasure of every fact, naturalists also embrace their lack of knowledge.

8　Observation is of no use to reduce ignorance since naturalists have already been adept in their fields.

9　Socrates knew nothing when young but he knew everything when old.

10　The philosophy of ignorance lies in an enquiring mind to ask, a fresh eye to see, and an awareness to self-reflect.

TEXT A The Pleasures of Ignorance

Robert Lynd

It is impossible to take a walk in the country with an average townsman—especially, perhaps, in April or May—without being amazed at the vast continent of his ignorance. It is impossible to take a walk in the country oneself without being amazed at the vast continent of one's own ignorance. Thousands of men and women live and die without knowing the difference between a **beech** and an **elm**, between the song of a **thrush** and the song of a **blackbird**. Probably in a modern city the man who can distinguish between a thrush's and a blackbird's song is the exception. It is not that we have not seen the birds. It is simply that we have not noticed them. We have been surrounded by birds all our lives, yet so **feeble** is our observation that many of us could not tell whether or not the **chaffinch** sings, or the colour of the **cuckoo**.

This ignorance, however, is not altogether miserable. Out of it we get the constant pleasure of discovery. Every fact of nature comes to us each spring, if only we are sufficiently ignorant, with the **dew** still on it. If we have lived half a lifetime without having ever even seen a cuckoo, and know it only as a wandering voice, we are all the more delighted at the **spectacle** of its runaway flight as it hurries from wood to wood conscious of its crimes, and at the way in which it **halts** hawk-like in the wind, its long tail **quivering**, before it dares descend on a hill-side of fir-trees where **avenging** presences may **lurk**.

It would be absurd to pretend that the **naturalist** does not also find pleasure in observing the life of the birds, but his is a steady pleasure, almost a **sober** and **plodding** occupation, compared to the morning enthusiasm of the man who sees a cuckoo for the first time. And, as to that, the happiness even of the naturalist depends in some measure upon his ignorance, which still leaves him new worlds of this kind to conquer. He may have reached the very Z of knowledge in the books, but he still feels half ignorant until he has confirmed each bright particular with his eyes. Assuredly the men of science have no reason as yet to weep over their lost ignorance. There will always be a fortune of ignorance waiting for them under every fact they turn up.

But your and my ignorance is not confined to cuckoos. It **dabbles** in all created things, from the sun and moon down to the names of the flowers, including nearly everything you and I have taken for granted. One of the greatest joys known to man is to take such a flight into ignorance in search of knowledge. The great pleasure of ignorance is, after all, the pleasure of asking questions. The man who has lost this pleasure or exchanged it for the pleasure of **dogma**, which is the pleasure of answering, is already beginning to **stiffen**. Do not forget that Socrates was famed for wisdom not because he was **omniscient** but because he realised at the age of seventy that he still knew nothing. Once more I shall see the world as a garden through the eyes of a stranger, my breath taken away with surprise by the painted fields.

Notes

1. ***The Pleasures of Ignorance***
   这一标题字面译为"无知的乐趣"。根据Collins Cobuild词典, "ignorance"(无知)一为贬义词, 意为"缺乏教养"; 二为中性词, 意为"不知晓、不知情"。此处作者采用了语义双关。从字面来看, 文章标题选取的是第一义项, 但实际上作者给"无知"的贬义义项赋予了正面积极的意义, 即由"无知"而产生的"求知"充满乐趣。

2. **Robert Lynd**
   Robert Lynd (1879–1949) was an Irish writer, a literary essayist. He edited the trade magazine *Publishers Weekly* and later worked for book-publishing firms in New York City. He directed a sociological study of small cities for the Institute of Social and Religious Research, and served as an official of the Social Science Research Council.

3. **Probably in a modern city the man who can distinguish between a thrush's and a blackbird's song is the exception. (Lines 6–8)**
   此处的"the exception"即只此例外, 强调此类人能够区分鸫和乌鸫的叫声, 为特例。注意"the exception"与"an exception"的区别, 后者表明例外中的一例。

4. **Socrates (Line 37)**
   Socrates (469–399 B.C.E.) was a Greek philosopher and is considered the father of Western philosophy. Unlike other figures of comparable importance, such as the Buddha or Confucius, he did not tell his audience how they should live. What Socrates taught was a method of questioning to arrive at the truth, also called Socratic Method, which laid the groundwork for Western systems of logic and philosophy.

STUDY READING

A Structure Analysis

Fill in each blank with no more than four words according to your understanding of the structure and content of the text.

The Pleasures of Ignorance	
Introduction (Para. 1)	When we take a walk in the country, we are amazed at the vast continent of (1) _____. We take for granted what we see each day or we (2) _____ them.
Body (Paras. 2–3)	This ignorance, however, is not altogether miserable; we get constant (3) _____ out of it. The naturalist finds steady pleasure in observing the life of the birds. Still, his ignorance leaves him (4) _____. Therefore, there will always be (5) _____.
Conclusion (Para. 4)	Basically, our ignorance is for (6) _____ we've taken for granted. And one of the greatest joys known to man lies in the (7) _____; the great pleasure of ignorance is the pleasure of (8) _____.

B Reading Comprehension

I Sequencing: Identify the order of the following statements according to the text.

_____ A People know about their ignorance whenever they go for a walk in the country.

_____ B Even naturalists with much knowledge can find pleasure in observing the life of the birds.

_____ C Not everyone can tell the difference between a thrush's song and a blackbird's song.

_____ D A philosopher was famous for his wisdom because he still realized his ignorance even when he was old.

_____ E People can get the pleasure of discovery from ignorance, which doesn't only cause misery.

_____ F Seeking knowledge from ignorance is one of the greatest joys to human beings.

II Blank Filling: Fill in each blank with no more than three words based on the text.

1. It is an exception that a man in the modern city can _____ the song of a thrush and a blackbird because most people are ignorant of nature.

2. If we have only known a cuckoo as a wandering voice, we will be _____ delighted when noticing that it flies away from wood to wood conscious of its crimes.

3. _____ the average people's enthusiasm about seeing a cuckoo for the first time, the pleasure of the naturalists is much more steady.

4. The happiness of a naturalist relies _____ on his ignorance because the new world is what he is going to explore.

5. Our ignorance _____ all things taken for granted by us, including the sun, the moon, the names of flowers, and other things from nature.

6. When we realize our ignorance _____ knowledge, we will gain great joy.

7. Socrates was _____ wisdom not because he knew everything but because he was aware of his ignorance.

8. Every time I observed the garden from a new perspective, my breath was _____ by the beautiful scene.

III Group Work: The famous Greek philosopher Socrates once said, "I know nothing except the fact of my ignorance," which is also known as "Socratic ignorance". Work in groups and have a discussion on the Socratic ignorance. After the discussion, a group member should be recommended to give a presentation.

WORD BUILDING

A Prefabs

Exercise 1 Blank Filling: Active Words

I Study the meanings of the active nouns, verbs and adjectives in the table.

Active Words

Title	**ignorance** /ˈɪgnərəns/ *n.*	[U] Ignorance of something is lack of knowledge about it.
12	**miserable** /ˈmɪzərəbl/ *adj.*	If you describe a place or situation as miserable, you mean that it makes you feel unhappy or depressed. *a miserable place*
14	**sufficient** /səˈfɪʃnt/ *adj.*	If something is sufficient for a particular purpose, there is enough of it for the purpose. *to be sufficient for photography without flash*
14	**ignorant** /ˈɪgnərənt/ *adj.* Adj *of* n	If someone is ignorant of a fact, he or she does not know it. *to be ignorant of the facts about global warming*
18	**descend** /dɪˈsend/ *vi.* V *on*	If a large group of people arrive to see you, especially if their visit is unexpected or causes you a lot of work, you can say that they have descended on you. *to be descending on the peaceful villages*
20	**absurd** /əbˈsɜːd/ *adj.*	If you say that something is absurd, you are criticizing it because you think that it is ridiculous or that it does not make sense. *to go to absurd lengths*
22	**enthusiasm** /ɪnˈθjuːziˌæzəm/ *n.*	[U] Enthusiasm is great eagerness to be involved in a particular activity which you like and enjoy or which you think is important.
25	**conquer** /ˈkɒŋkə(r)/ *vt.* V n	If you conquer something such as a problem, you succeed in ending it or dealing with it successfully. *to conquer our differences*
26	**confirm** /kənˈfɜːm/ *vt.* V n	If you confirm something that has been stated or suggested, you say that it is true because you know about it. *to confirm what had long been feared*
27	**assure** /əˈʃʊə(r)/ *vt.* V n	If you assure someone that something is true or will happen, you tell him or her that it is definitely true or will definitely happen. *to assure me that there was nothing traumatic*
30	**confine** /kənˈfaɪn/ *vt.* V n *to* n	To confine something to a particular place or group means to prevent it from spreading beyond that place or group. *to confine the epidemic to the area*
37	**famed** /feɪmd/ *adj.* be Adj *for*	If people, places, or things are famed for a particular thing, they are very well known for it. *to be famed for its beauty*

II **Now complete the sentences with the words in the table above. You need to change the form where necessary.**

1. Thousands of mainstream web developers _____ on Austin Texas for five days of seminars, discussions and interaction—all with a goal of making the web a better place for all users.

2. In my view, his evidence is clearly _____, unreasonable, and not remotely believable.

3. As a mathematician Carlyle is _____ for his English translation of Legendre's *Eléments de Géométrie*.

4. The 80-year-old has since posted regular messages and photos on social media to _____ fans that he is recovering well.

5. Almost all of the twice-married people lamented (痛惜) their _____ and inexperience the first time they married.

6. Illegal workers have to accept terribly low wages, _____ working conditions, and essentially no benefits.

7. They chose teaching as a career because they loved their subject and wanted to share their _____ with others.

8. In Britain "please" is not _____ to one sort of politeness. Many or most say "please" in all situations because they were trained to do so long before they could understand why.

9. It is the duty of society to produce a(n) _____ quantity of food to nourish everyone in the world.

10. He is a role model who _____ adversity, remained in school, and now looks forward to a promising future.

11. I would really like to see a robust and non-biased calculation to truly _____ the limited data I have seen.

12. Some argue that we are the largest science experiment ever to take place, as we are _____ of the side effects of genetically modified food.

Exercise 2   Prefab Translation

I   Discuss the meanings of the following prefabs in the text.

Prefabs

9	all one's life	24	in some measure
15	half a lifetime	27	as yet
16	all the more	28	weep over
16	at the spectacle of	30	be confined to
23	for the first time	33	in search of

II   Translate the following into English, using the prefabs in the table above.

1   激发一个人生命中的各种潜能   _____

2   因投资失败浪费了半生的光阴   _____

3   找到了更加喜欢英语的理由   _____

4   看到特大火灾的情景泪奔了   _____

5   第一次遇到真正的竞争对手   _____

6   多多少少提高了阅读理解能力   _____

7   至今尚未得到任何正式答复   _____

8   为失去爱妻而伤心地痛哭   _____

9   积劳成疾，卧床不起   _____

10   寻思多日以求解答这一问题   _____

B Partial Dictation

Listen to the following sentences once only and fill in the blanks with the exact words you hear.

1. Many people _____ a beech from an elm throughout their life.

2. For the man in a modern city, a thrush's song and a blackbird's song _____.

3. With its long tail quivering, a cuckoo _____ in the wind like a hawk, before it dares descend on a hill-side of fir-trees.

4. The naturalist's pleasure in observing the life of the birds is a stable one _____ the morning enthusiasm of the man who sees a cuckoo for the first time.

5. Even though a person has _____ in the books, he still feels half ignorant until he has confirmed each bright particular in person.

6. Human beings' ignorance is not _____ cuckoos and it is a common phenomenon.

7. People's ignorance _____ nearly everything in the world that we have taken for granted.

8. One of _____ is to take a flight into ignorance in search of knowledge.

C Sentence Translation

Translate the Chinese sentences into English, using the expressions in the brackets.

1. 通常情况下，人类生存和死亡的状况是由政治、社会和经济因素决定的。(*live and die*)

2. 我们不要终日纠结于利弊得失的问题，而是要努力加快经济发展的步子。(*distinguish between*)

3. 粉丝们等了半天也不见电影明星露脸。(*turn up*)

4. 瑞士以风景优美著名，有山有湖，空气清新。(*be famed for*)

5. 人类对于造成这种疾病的原因迄今一无所知。(*know nothing*)

Translation Tips

From a Bird's Song to Animal Voices

In Para. 1 of the text, one of the sentences reads: "Probably in a modern city the man who can distinguish between a thrush's and a blackbird's <u>song</u> is the exception." One may translate the underlined word "song" into Chinese "歌声". To be exact, the word "song" in this context, referring to the voice of a bird, had better be rendered into Chinese "叫声". Thus, the whole sentence could be understood in Chinese as "或许现代都市中能分辨鸫和乌鸫叫声的人就是特例了".

This case in point cautions a translator on the proper collocations in terms of animal voices. In the Chinese language, the verb "叫" or its noun "叫声" is applicable for almost all animals in making up a phrase or sentence. However, this is not the case with animal voices in the English language. For example, a tiger "roars", but a cat "meows"; a wolf "howls" while a dog "barks"; a bird "sings", whereas a frog "croaks".

Special collocations for some animal voices are selected below to help keep the students from translation errors.

Animal Names		Animal Voices	Examples
Chinese	English		
百灵鸟	lark	sing	百灵鸟在不停地叫。The lark kept singing.
公鸡	rooster	crow	那只公鸡早上5点就开始叫了，把我们都吵醒了。The rooster started to crow at five in the morning and woke us all.
狗	dog	bark	会叫的狗不咬人。A barking dog never bites.
海鸥	seagull	mew	海鸥在港湾上空鸣叫。The seagulls mewed over the bay.
猴子	monkey	screech	猴子在山上叫。The monkeys screeched in the mountain.
老虎	tiger	roar	听到远处老虎的叫声 hear a tiger roaring in the distance
狼	wolf	howl	狼叫了一声。The wolf gave a howl.
马	horse	neigh	马儿开始叫了起来。The horse started neighing.
猫	cat	meow	猫饿得直叫，我们就把它放了进来。The hungry cat meowed and we let it in.
母鸡	hen	cluck	母鸡下完蛋后叫个不停。The hen kept clucking after it laid an egg.
青蛙	frog	croak	青蛙呱呱地叫。A frog croaks.
狮子	lion	roar	像一头吼叫着的狮子 like a roaring lion
鸭子	duck	quack	小河上一群鸭子在嘎嘎地叫。A flock of ducks was quacking on the small river.
羊	sheep	bleat	他们把这头叫个不停的羊放了进去。They let the bleating sheep in.
鹰	eagle; hawk	scream	鹰刺耳的尖叫把她吓得毛骨悚然。The hawk's piercing scream curdled her blood.
知了	cicada	chirp	知了在树上叫了一整天。The cicadas have been chirping in the trees all day.
猪	pig	grunt	猪吓得咕噜咕噜叫起来，都逃走了。The pigs fled in grunting alarm.

GRAMMARING

A *may/might, could, must + perfect infinitive*

We use "modal + perfect infinitive" to talk about varying degrees of certainty about past events.

Meanings	Examples
possibility	■ He *may have reached* the very Z of knowledge in the books, but he still feels half ignorant until he has confirmed each bright particular with his eyes. ■ You *could have done* better, but you didn't try your best.
certainty	■ The car driver *must have panicked* when he saw the buses moving in on both sides.

- We use *can't have done / couldn't have done* to express impossibilities in the past.
- We use *could have done*, but not *can have done* to express an opinion or suggestion for a past option.
- The opposite of *must have done* is *can't have done*.

I Complete the sentences with the appropriate forms of the verbs given in the brackets.

1. There was only one thing you could _____ (do) to prevent losing it. And you have done it.

2. It halts hawk-like in the wind before it dares descend on a hill-side of fir-trees where avenging presences may _____ (lurk).

3. What a shame! With a bit more effort we might _____ (win) the match.

4. It can _____ (be) dangerous to cycle in the city.

5. He is not likely to be the kind of man who could _____ (do) such a rude thing to a lady. You must _____ (be) mistaken.

6. She can't _____ (leave) the house yet because her car is still outside.

II Complete the conversations, using the modals and verbs and phrase given in the box. Change the form where necessary.

might record	could forget	must fail	can't do	couldn't throw away	might not

1. **A:** John didn't turn up for the meeting.
   B: He _____ that we were meeting today.

2   **A:** I'm sorry. I didn't make it.
    B: Oh well, you did the best you _____.

3   **A:** I just don't believe that Andy has failed the algebra exam.
    B: Andy? Impossible! He _____.

4   **A:** Did you record the program?
    B: I can't remember. I _____.

5   **A:** Can't you find the newspaper?
    B: No, someone _____.

B prepositions in relative clauses

A relative pronoun can be the object of a preposition. In formal English, the preposition comes at the beginning of the relative clause, before *which* or *whom*. For example:

- We are all the more delighted at the way *in which* it halts hawk-like in the wind, its long tail quivering.
- The sales manager is the person *from whom* I obtained the figures.

In informal spoken English, we normally put the preposition at the end of the relative clause, and often leave out the relative pronoun. For example:

- I can't remember the name of the hotel *we stayed at*.

I Rewrite the following sentences so that they are more appropriate for the formal written style.

1 The social group we are referring to is the upper middle class.

2 The firm that he used to work for has now been forced to close down.

3 The book is enjoyed by adults, as well as children, who it was primarily written for.

4 This is the statement I cannot agree with.

5 Allowing the weapons to be sold is an action the government should be ashamed of.

6 The dragonfly is an insect that we know very little of.

II Fill in the blanks with prepositions.

1 The date _____ which applications should be sent is January 1st.

2 The rate _____ which a material heats up depends on its chemical composition.

3 The lawyers examined a large number of documents, _____ which they discovered the contract.

4 I would like to thank my tutor, _____ whom I would never have finished the work.

5 I then turn to Einstein, _____ whose work the following quotation is taken.

6 The house _____ which Mozart was born is now a museum.

7 The headmaster, _____ whom the parents had discussed the son's future, advised the boy to take up engineering.

8 Draw a circle, the radius _____ which is one inch.

9 Can you describe a situation _____ which two very different varieties of language co-exist in a speech community?

10 The mid-19th century was a period _____ which many people left Ireland.

C genitive -'s

The genitive can be used to talk about possession, relationship, physical features, non-physical qualities and measurement.

We are more likely to use the -'s:	We are more likely to use the *of*-phrase:
• when the noun refers to living things, especially a person or a group of people. ■ *Dan's* dream for a bicycle came true on his birthday.	• with an inanimate noun; ■ the names *of the flowers* • when the noun phrase is a long one, especially one with a postmodifier. ■ the morning enthusiasm *of the man who sees a cuckoo for the first time*

With hyphenated or compound words, we add -'s to the last element.

■ my sister-in-law's advice

With a coordinated noun phrase,

• if there is a joint possession, we add -'s to the last noun;

■ Mike and Amanda's new loft apartment is really neat.

• if there is a separate possession of the same thing, we add -'s to each of the nouns.

■ a thrush's and a blackbird's song

I Rewrite the sentences, using genitive -'s.

1 The house belonging to that man is the red wooden one.
   _____ is the red wooden one.

2 The discoveries made by Mme Curie helped to shape the discipline and profession of chemistry.
   _____ helped to shape the discipline and profession of chemistry.

3 The stories Sam told were completely different from the stories Pauline told.
   _____ were completely different.

4 Troubles in life can sometimes leave us with a frown.
   _____ can sometimes leave us with a frown.

5 Annie and Mary will be late getting home from school. Please tell their mother.
   Please tell _____ that they'll be late getting home from school.

6 The book is about the great adventure of discovery that Lewis and Clark went on.
   The book is about _____.

II Complete the sentences with the -'s form or *of*-phrase of the words in the brackets.

1 _____ (each day / worries) can get us down.

2 As announced in _____ (newspaper/today), a new satellite has been launched.

3 Our organization strives towards _____ (poverty/elimination).

4 We need to work together to make all the _____ (world/problems) disappear.

5 We believe that _____ (today/science) is _____ (tomorrow/technology).

6 _____ (industry/development) has been a gradual process throughout human existence, from stone tools to modern technology.

> *Of*-phrase is used when *today, yesterday, tomorrow, the day* are used to mean present, past, future, this (that) time.

COMMUNICATING

A Viewing: Happy Elephants

I Get Prepared: Look at the photos and answer the questions.

1 Where do you think elephants may be happier, in captivity or in the wild?
   _____

2 What can you see in Photos 2 and 4?
   _____

3 What do you think the man is doing in Photo 4?
   _____

II Get Prepared: You will hear these proper names and words and expressions in the video. Read aloud the proper names in Table 1. Then study the words and expressions in Table 2.

Table 1	Proper Names
Mike Hackenberger	人名
Baltimore	巴尔的摩（美国马里兰州最大城市）
Fatman	大象名
Funnyface	大象名
Limba	大象名
Quebec	魁北克（加拿大省名）

Table 2	Words and Expressions
in the wild	在野外；野生的
in captivity	囚禁；圈养的
ingrown	向内生长的
husbandry	畜牧管理
barbaric	野蛮的
herd	牧群

III Watch and Listen for Gist: Watch the video and circle the correct answer to the question.

▶ 1.03

How can people keep elephants happy in zoos?

a. Feed them with watermelons.

b. Keep them in cages or chain them up.

c. Train them to be what they are in the wild.

IV Watch and Listen for Details: Watch ▶ 1.03 again and circle the correct answers.

1 The one question about elephants that people discuss a lot is: _____

   a. Can elephants be happy?

   b. Are animals as happy as children?

   c. Are elephants happier in circuses than in zoos?

Unit 1 Ignorance 17

2 Most people who work with animals think that animals _____.

   a. cannot have feelings

   b. have feelings

   c. are always happy

3 Which is NOT one way that Hackenberger tries to make his elephants healthy and happy?

   a. He checks their feet and teeth.

   b. He talks to them.

   c. He takes them to circuses.

4 In modern society, _____ animal training techniques are no longer used.

   a. easy

   b. good

   c. unkind

5 Why did Limba love the young elephants?

   a. Because elephants love all young animals.

   b. Because elephants are social animals.

   c. Because young elephants are gentler than older ones.

6 Which of the following is something elephants do in the wild?

   a. Swim and play in the mud.

   b. Communicate with humans.

   c. Play together with trainers.

V Watch and Infer Information: Watch part of the video and circle the correct answer.

What does Hackenberger believe about making elephants happy in captivity?

a. Elephants can't be happy in a zoo.

b. Elephants are happy anywhere they can be just elephants.

c. Elephants can only be happy in captivity if they have a good trainer.

VI **Watch and Listen for Language Use:** Watch part of the video and fill in the blanks with the exact words you hear.

▶ 1.05

Elephants are (1) _____. (2) _____ that they live in families and (3) _____ and they need other elephants. If they are alone for a long time, elephants can start to (4) _____.

Hackenberger talks about one elephant called Limba. Limba was alone for 30 years in a zoo in northern Quebec. She didn't (5) _____. Hackenberger then tells how two other elephants (6) _____ Limba when they were only two days old. Limba (7) _____ the two young elephants, he explains, and (8) _____ she became a happier and (9) _____ elephant.

When he's training elephants, Hackenberger (10) _____ _____, and there's one thing elephants love.

B Speaking

Activity 1   Can Animals Think like Humans Do?

I Complete the conversation by filling in the blanks with appropriate expressions. Then listen and check your answers.

🎧 1.06

Yuki: Animals are interesting. They can be trained to do many things, but can they think like humans do?

Min: (1) _____. But I do know that some animals are intelligent.

Yuki: Oh, yes. Parrots can imitate human speech. But (2) _____ whether they can think like we humans do.

Min: They are no doubt smart birds—they can even sing human songs!

Yuki: That's true. But are they happy like humans when they sing a happy song?

Min: (3) _____. I saw a video clip some time ago. This bird seemed to be very happy while singing a song.

Yuki: (4) _____.

Min: It's true! I can show you the video. Here, on my mobile, see for yourself!

Yuki: Wow! That's incredible! But I'm still (5) _____ about that. I think we need to do some research to know more about animals.

II **Pair Work:** Practice the conversation with a partner.

III Read the useful expressions aloud.

Useful Expressions for Showing Degrees of Certainty			
Do animals have feelings? / Are they happy?			
very certain	less certain	not very certain	not certain at all
■ Yes, they do/are. ■ No, they don't/aren't.	■ I think they do/are. ■ I don't think they do/are.	■ Maybe. I'm not sure. ■ I'm doubtful about it.	■ I have no idea. ■ I don't know.

IV Pair Work: Read the questions below. Add your own question for each topic. Then take turns asking and answering the questions with a partner. Use the expressions above to help you.

Your Teacher	Your Best Friend	Your Pet
■ Is your teacher strict? ■ Does your teacher like playing football? Your question: _____	■ Does your best friend smoke? ■ Does your best friend live near you? Your question: _____	■ Does your pet eat vegetables? ■ Is your pet mild? Your question: _____
Your School	**Your Dormitory**	**Your Mobile**
■ Are there a lot of restaurants near your school? ■ Is there a high-speed railway station near your school? Your question: _____	■ Is your dormitory always tidy and clean? ■ Does your dormitory have air conditioning? Your question: _____	■ Does your mobile use 5G technology? ■ Is your mobile made in China? Your question: _____

> Is your mobile made in China?

> Yes, it is. It is made by a major Chinese company. How about yours?

> Same here. Does your phone use the latest technology?

> Yes, it does. The maker is always the leader in this field, you know.

Unit 1 **Ignorance**

Activity 2 How Much Do You Know About the Human Brain?

I Read the information about the human brain in the chart. Add your own findings.

Some Facts About the Human Brain
About 75% of our brain is made up of water.
It weighs approximately 1.5 kg and represents 2% to 3% of our body mass.
It consumes about 20% of our oxygen.
It is capable of storing the equivalent of 1,000 terabytes of information.
It has more connections than the number of stars in our galaxy.
The shape of our brains can reveal a lot about our behavior and the risks of developing mental disorders.
Very few people have the ability to affect objects or living beings at a certain distance, solely through the power of the mind, without using any kind of physical force.
Your findings:

II **Group Work:** Use the information in the chart above and discuss our brains with your partners. You may use the model dialog for help.

A: It's impossible to talk about the power of the human brain without knowing something about it.

B: Sure. I don't know much about my own brain. Sometimes I'm just amazed at my ignorance.

C: Relax! It's not that we haven't thought about it. It is simply that we haven't done enough research to discover more about what is going on in our brains.

A: You made a point. According to scientists, about 75% of our brain is made up of water.

C: And it weighs approximately 1.5 kg and represents 2% to 3% of our body mass.

D: It consumes about 20% of our oxygen.

B: No wonder I feel dizzy when I think hard, especially when I can't figure out a solution to a difficult problem.

D: Using the brain costs oxygen!

C Writing

I Fill in the blanks with phrases from the box to complete the paragraphs. You may need to make necessary changes to some of the phrases.

> be amazed at
> It is not that / It is simply that
> be delighted at
> in some measure
> the men of science
> be confined to
>
> distinguish between… and
> the difference between… and…
> find pleasure in
> the very Z of knowledge
> a fortune of
> in search of

All of us are ignorant to some extent if we are in an entirely new realm. In "Of Gardening", Bacon holds that there should be different kinds of plants and flowers in season to make gardens as beautiful as possible. We may (1) _____ our own ignorance when required to name such green plants and flowers in the season of winter as holly (冬青), ivy (常春藤), rosemary (迷迭香), lavender (薰衣草), germander (石蚕花), etc. The rudimentary knowledge most of us have about winter plants (2) _____ such plants as cypress-trees (柏树), yew trees (紫杉), pine trees (松树), fir-trees (冷杉). Some of us even fail to tell (3) _____ cypress-trees _____ pine trees, and between yew trees and fir-trees.

However, this ignorance is not altogether miserable. Out of it we get the constant pleasure of knowing something new. For instance, perhaps we are beginning to acquire some knowledge about such plants and flowers as different kinds of roses, honeysuckles (忍冬), strawberries, the French marigold (法国万寿菊), figs in fruit (挂果无花果树), vine-flowers (葡萄花), etc. when we are (4) _____ those that come into season in May and June.

A beautiful garden is of course pleasant to the eye. If we have sufficient knowledge to (5) _____ similar plants _____ flowers, we are likely to (6) _____ the variety of plants and flowers. In this particular sense, the degree of our pleasure and happiness depends (7) _____ on how much knowledge we have about them.

II Now write an essay of about 220 words on *Ignorance and Knowledge*. You may use the phrases from the box above.

TEXT B — Viewing Nature's Beauty Through a New Lens

Sonia Harmon

Filmmaker Louie Schwartzberg has shot everything from TV **commercials** to **documentaries**, but he is best known for his **time-lapse photography**, a technique that captures images on film very slowly. When shown at regular speed, the viewer can see things the human eye cannot normally see. Schwartzberg's remarkable documentary—*Mysteries of the Unseen World*—illustrates his talent for capturing the wonders of nature using this technique.

National Geographic spoke with Louie Schwartzberg about the challenges and rewards of his career in photography, the issues he feels most **passionate** about, and why he believes it's important that we all become more connected to nature.

How did you become interested in nature photography and filmmaking?

I found my voice with photography as a student at UCLA (the University of California at Los Angeles). We had anti-war **protests** going on right outside my classroom, so I picked up a camera and started to document that. And when I met my greatest teacher, I fell in love with nature. He taught me everything about lighting, composition, color, and how to live a **sustainable**, creative life.

Can you explain a little more about your Moving Art project and what the mission is?

Basically, I've got a thousand hours of material that I've filmed over the years. The mission is to be able to share how cool nature is—there's amazing time-lapse, slow motion, and **aerials**. You may have heard of nature **deficit** disorder, where kids are suffering from the fact that they're not connected to nature, but

I think what we need to do is engage them where they are. That's what I'm trying to do.

You've been shooting time-lapse 24/7 for over three decades. What have you been shooting?

Flowers, primarily. They kind of seduce you with their beauty and you fall in love with them. That's why I made a film about pollination, which is so critical. A third of our food comes from pollinating plants. But to answer your question specifically, I've got two cameras going nonstop 24 hours a day, 7 days a week, because time is precious and I don't want to waste a single second. I've squeezed 35 years of shooting into 12 hours of material.

What are some of the challenges that you deal with when you're time-lapse filmmaking?

The biggest ones, I think, are mosquitoes. They come out at sunset, at early dawn, and at twilight... but besides the mosquitoes, when I'm on location, it's about survival. I've got to figure out food, water, transportation, and how to get back home when it gets dark. It's not just the technique, but I do it because I think time-lapse can transform your consciousness by helping you see things from a different point of view. That's when you change your perspective. And when you change your perspective, that's how you develop gratitude.

What's one of the most memorable experiences you've had in nature while doing your work?

I was recently in Panama shooting hummingbirds in slow motion. It's just amazing to see their world. They're very territorial with the way they kind of fight each other to get the flower. And nectar-feeding bats in the Sonoran Desert—I got this incredible shot of a baby bat breastfeeding on the mother bat as the mom is feeding on a flower in the desert. Most people don't realize the entire Sonoran Desert would not exist without these nectar-feeding bats.

What environmental issues mean the most to you right now?

I think [bee] colony collapse disorder would be at the top. I've heard scientists say it could be way more serious than climate change. And there's a quote attributed to Einstein that if the bees ever disappeared, man would only have four years left to live. It doesn't really matter whether it's true or whether Einstein said

---

seduce *vt.* 诱惑

pollination *n.* 授粉作用

squeeze *vt.* 挤压；好不容易取得

twilight *n.* 黄昏

hummingbird *n.* 蜂鸟

territorial *adj.* 领地的
nectar-feeding *adj.* 吸蜜性的

colony collapse disorder 蜂群崩溃综合征
attribute *vt.* 把……归于

it or not. The healthiest food we need to eat—fruits, nuts, seeds, and vegetables—would disappear without pollinating plants. It's pretty serious.

70 What would you say is one of the most surprising things you've learned in your career?

I keep getting the same things **reinforced** over and over. When I film things, I'm connecting with the universal rhythms of the universe, which is the deepest part of my soul. And it's 75 this constant reminder that it's all connected. I also think we always have to be curious, and nature really inspires you to be an explorer. To be an explorer and to be a scientist is the same idea; it's all about curiosity. And I think the same thing is true being a filmmaker or an artist. We have different rules, but we're 80 both trying to share the wonders of nature and the universe with people.

reinforce *vt.* 加强

Notes

1. **Sonia Harmon**

   Sonia Harmon is a blog coordinator at National Geographic, a global nonprofit organization which has reached three million readers each year and engaged audience all over the world. She has also written for other magazines, including *Washingtonian* and *Ladies Home Journal*.

2. **Louie Schwartzberg (Line 1)**

   Louie Schwartzberg is an award-winning director, producer and cinematographer. Using time-lapse, high-speed and macro cinematography techniques, he provided us with unprecedented photos.

3. **nature deficit disorder (Line 26)**

   First coined by journalist Richard Louv in 2005, nature deficit disorder refers to a trend in which people, especially children are lack of touch with nature. It exerts an influence on their behavior in negative ways, making them fail to achieve a peaceful mind and happiness.

4. **colony collapse disorder (Line 62)**

   Colony collapse disorder, abbreviated as CCD, is a phenomenon that the majority of adult worker bees in a colony suddenly disappear. The reason still remains unknown. In recent years, the reported cases have declined substantially.

EXERCISES

A Reading for Gist

Answer the following questions according to your understanding of Text B.

1 According to the text, what is unique about the "time-lapse photography"?

_____

_____

2 What inspired Louie Schwartzberg to devote himself to nature photograph and filmmaking?

_____

_____

B Reading for Details

Each of the following statements contains information given in the text. Identify and write down the corresponding number of the paragraph from which the information is derived.

1 I aim to demonstrate the charm of nature and change the situation that kids are less exposed to nature.   Para. _____

2 It was my stroke of luck to meet my teacher, who guided me to learn professional techniques in photography and opened my world of documenting nature.   Para. _____

3 It's impressive to discover the world where hummingbirds live.   Para. _____

4 Scientists and explorers share the same quality: curiosity.   Para. _____

5 It's of great significance to protect bees that play an indispensable role in pollinating plants.   Para. _____

C Reading Beyond

Discuss with your group members the following topic for about 15 minutes. Then share your opinions with the whole class.

Topic: What environmental issue means the most to you right now? And why?

D Prefabs

Write the Chinese meanings of the following prefabs in the text.

at regular speed   _____

feel passionate about   _____

become more connected to   _____

fall in love with   _____

slow motion   _____

seduce sb. with sth.   _____

be on location   _____

see sth. from a different point of view   _____

at the top   _____

climate change   _____

E Sentence Translation

I Translate the English sentences into Chinese.

1 He taught me everything about lighting, composition, color, and how to live a sustainable, creative life.

2 The mission is to be able to share how cool nature is—there's amazing time-lapse, slow motion, and aerials.

3 We have different rules, but we're both trying to share the wonders of nature and the universe with people.

II Translate the Chinese sentences into English, using the expressions in the brackets.

1 据说上海最负盛名的是东方明珠广播电视塔。(*best known*)

2 这部电影全部是在英法等欧洲国家实景拍摄的。(*on location*)

3 医生建议病人最好吃一段时间粗粮。(*feed on*)

Unit 2 Communication

Warming Up

Memorize and comment on the following quotations on communication.

1 与人善言,暖于布帛;伤人之言,深于矛戟。

——《荀子·荣辱》

2 People fail to get along because they fear each other; they fear each other because they don't know each other; they don't know each other because they have not communicated with each other.

— Martin Luther King, Jr.

INITIAL READING

A Vocabulary

Read the new words aloud and try to work out their meanings in the text.

New Words

Title	**communicator** /kəˈmjuːnɪkeɪtə(r)/ n.	30	**feature** /ˈfiːtʃə(r)/ n.
11	**encode** /ɪnˈkəʊd/ vt.	37	**strive** /straɪv/ vi.
14	**decode** /diːˈkəʊd/ vt.	37	**clarity** /ˈklærəti/ n.
15	**transmission** /trænzˈmɪʃn/ n.	41	**facilitate** /fəˈsɪlɪteɪt/ vt.
15	**straightforward** /ˌstreɪtˈfɔːwəd/ adj.	42	**terminology** /ˌtɜːmɪˈnɒlədʒi/ n.
23	**range** /reɪndʒ/ n.	45	**external** /ɪkˈstɜːnl/ adj.
29	**tailor** /ˈteɪlə(r)/ vt.	46	**multicultural** /ˌmʌltiˈkʌltʃərəl/ adj.
29	**mode** /məʊd/ n.	55	**objective** /əbˈdʒektɪv/ n.

B Skimming

Read Text A and go through the statements within eight minutes. Circle the numbers of the correct statements.

1. Good communicative skills are the most important for businesspeople.
2. People should cultivate good commutative skills because they can improve the overall performance at work.
3. Communication takes different forms, all of which require interaction with one another.
4. A sender usually decodes the message he or she wants to convey before sending it to the receiver.
5. The receiver interprets the message only based on the words he or she hears.
6. Noise is inevitable during the communication process.
7. People can improve business communicative skills by following certain principles.
8. One should always keep the audience in mind while preparing for his or her speech.
9. Organizational culture has nothing to do with business communication.
10. The only purpose of effective business communication is to build a long-lasting relationship with partners.

TEXT A: How to Become an Effective Communicator in a Business Context

Varun Mittal

What is so important about good communication? Communication helps build effective relationships with colleagues and business partners. It helps you become a better team player, contribute more to innovative projects, influence decisions, and get your ideas and proposals accepted. It helps employers improve and manage relationships with customers and resolve conflict. Good communication helps to make the most of opportunities.

Every form of communication requires interacting with another person or group of people—your audience.

It helps to imagine communication as an exchange of messages between a sender and a receiver through a medium or channel of communication. A message is **encoded** by the sender through sounds, written words, images, video, spoken language or body language, for example gestures, facial expressions and tone of voice. The message then reaches the receiver—the audience—who **decodes** it and may decide to respond.

This **transmission** of messages is not always **straightforward**, however. While the receiver hears or sees the message, a series of problems acting as "noise", may limit his or her ability to understand or assimilate it. These problems include the way the message is expressed, issues with the technology used, the receiver's inability to process the message and a lack of common ground (e.g., cultural factors such as values, beliefs and language) between the sender and the receiver. In some cases, when a common background isn't shared, the people involved need to work hard to build a mutual understanding and, therefore, exchange several messages or use a **range** of different media.

The following key principles of business communication will help you to get a message across to your receiver. They are:

Understand your audience

It is important to understand and be aware of your audience. They are the people you talk and write to. You should **tailor** the content and the **mode** of communication to suit their **features**. These include their interests and beliefs, background, roles and personalities.

Assuming that they will share your views and your background knowledge may lead to misunderstandings; therefore, it is important to prepare thoroughly before communicating with people you have just met and who may be from a different context. This will help you to not only achieve your present goal, but also to build or enhance your business relationships.

Strive for clarity

To be effective, your message must be clear. However, what is clear to you (the sender) may not be to the receiver, due to your different backgrounds. This is why following a standard way to write a report, organize a meeting or give a presentation, for example, can facilitate communication. Following standard grammatical rules and terminology also helps to produce a message that is clear to your audience.

Understand the context of your communication

When communicating for business purposes, you need to be aware of the culture of your organization and that of each department or external organization with which you communicate. Being mindful of the broader multicultural context of your audience is essential too. Without this understanding, you will not be able to establish common ground and understand each other.

Have a clear purpose in mind

The main reason to communicate in a business context is to achieve a specific purpose.

Whether you want to simply inform your audience or go about persuading them, make sure you know what you want them to understand and do. Think also of the relationship you have with your audience and how you want this to develop as a result of your communications. In some cases, building a good long-term relationship with a colleague or business partner may be your main objective. Whatever your purpose, if it is clear to you, you'll have a better chance of making it clear to them.

Notes

1. **Varun Mittal**
   Varun Mittal is a Search Engine Optimization (SEO) specialist at Honeywell Gurgaon, India. He is skilled in digital marketing, brand management, marketing management, sales, business development, marketing communication, consumer insights, market research, brand awareness, etc.

2. **body language (Line 12)**
   As part of nonverbal language, body language is the unspoken element of communication that we use to reveal our true feelings and emotions. It includes gestures, facial expressions, posture, and even small things that are barely perceptible like a brief shrug of the shoulder or nod of the head. It can strongly color how an individual is perceived, and how he or she, in turn, interprets others' motivation, mood, and openness.

3. **To be effective, your message… (Line 38)**
   不定式结构此处充当目的状语。

4. **… that of each department or external organization (Line 45)**
   "that" 此处用来替代 "the culture"。在英语的并列结构中，前后两项的名词相同而定语不同时，第二项的名词不能省略，常用 "that/those" 来替代。

STUDY READING

A Structure Analysis

Fill in each blank with no more than four words according to your understanding of the structure and content of the text.

	How to Become an Effective Communicator in a Business Context
What & Why (Paras. 1–4)	Good communication helps build (1) _____ with business partners and make the most of opportunities. Each form of communication requires interacting with your (2) _____. It is a sender-receiver (3) _____ via various media. However, this transmission is not always (4) _____ due to problems like the way the message is expressed, issues with technology, the receiver's inability and lack of common ground between the sender and the receiver.
How (Paras. 5–11)	Transition (Para. 5): The following principles will help you understand your receiver in a business context. • Understand your audience (Paras. 6–7): Be aware of your audience and (5) _____ the content and the mode of communication to suit their features. • Strive for (6) _____ (Para. 8): Follow a standard way when you write a report, organize a meeting or give a presentation. • Understand the context (Para. 9): Establish (7) _____ by understanding the context of your communication. • Have (8) _____ in mind (Paras. 10–11): Whatever your purpose is, make it clear to your audience.

B Reading Comprehension

I Sequencing: Identify the order of the following statements according to the text.

_____ A Understanding your audience means adjusting the content and mode of communication to their features.

_____ B You should also think of what the relationship with your audience is like after communication.

_____ C Messages are transmitted via various media: sounds, words, images, etc.

_____ D Good communication makes it easier for employers to improve their relationships with customers and reach an agreement.

_____ E People without a shared background have to work hard for mutual understanding.

_____ F Writing a report or giving a presentation in a standard way makes messages clear to the audience.

II Blank Filling: Fill in each blank with no more than three words based on the text.

1. Good communication is so important that it can help one to _____ of opportunities.
2. Communication means that one has to _____ the audience.
3. When there's no _____ between the sender and the receiver, the transmission of messages will not be straightforward.
4. The sender may _____ the message _____ if he or she masters some key principles in business communication.
5. The content and the mode of one's communication should be _____ suit the audience's features.
6. Due to different backgrounds, following a standard way can _____ communication.
7. In addition to the culture of one's organization, it is essential to _____ the broader multicultural context of the audience.
8. Before _____ persuading the audience, one should have a clear purpose in mind.

III Group Work: Are you an effective communicator at school? Work in groups and discuss effective communication skills. After the discussion, make a group presentation in front of the whole class.

WORD BUILDING

A Prefabs

Exercise 1 Blank Filling: Active Words

I Study the meanings of the active nouns, verbs and adjectives in the table.

Active Words

Title	**context** /ˈkɒntekst/ *n.*	[C] The context of an idea or event is the general situation that relates to it, and which helps it to be understood. *the historical context*
3	**contribute** /kənˈtrɪbjuːt/ *vi.* V *to*	If you contribute to something, you say or do things to help to make it successful. *to contribute to the family business*
3	**innovative** /ˈɪnəveɪtɪv/ *adj.*	Something that is innovative is new and original. *innovative products*
4	**proposal** /prəˈpəʊzl/ *n.*	[C] A proposal is a plan or an idea, often a formal or written one, which is suggested for people to think about and decide upon.
6	**conflict** /ˈkɒnflɪkt/ *n.*	[U] Conflict is serious disagreement or argument about something important. If two people or groups are in conflict, they have had a serious disagreement or argument and have not yet reached agreement.
7	**interact** /ˌɪntərˈækt/ *vi.* V *with*	When people interact with each other, they communicate as they work or spend time together. *to help parents interact with their babies*
11	**image** /ˈɪmɪdʒ/ *n.*	[C] An image is a picture of someone or something.
20	**factor** /ˈfæktə(r)/ *n.*	[C] A factor is one of the things that affects an event, decision, or situation.
22	**mutual** /ˈmjuːtʃuəl/ *adj.*	You use mutual to describe a situation, feeling, or action that is experienced, felt, or done by both of two people mentioned. *mutual benefit and progress*
47	**essential** /ɪˈsenʃl/ *adj.*	Something that is essential is extremely important or absolutely necessary to a particular subject, situation, or activity.
47	**establish** /ɪˈstæblɪʃ/ *vt.* V n	If someone establishes something such as an organization, a type of activity, or a set of rules, he or she creates it or introduces it in such a way that it is likely to last for a long time. *to establish detailed criteria*
50	**specific** /spəˈsɪfɪk/ *adj.*	You use specific to refer to a particular fixed area, problem, or subject. *specific problems to be dealt with*

Unit 2 **Communication**

II **Now complete the sentences with the words in the table above. You need to change the form where necessary.**

1. To write a good book review, it is important to establish some _____ for the book, situating it against some social or cultural backdrop.

2. Many _____ projects have a relatively low probability of success and may turn in profits over a longer time frame than conventional financing institutions expect.

3. I was worried that, for instance, there might be cultural _____ that would affect its success that didn't have anything to do with the school system.

4. The aim was to forge a(n) _____ understanding, one that could benefit both sides and end the violence that has been constant here for decades.

5. They believe it is _____ to show that the course of human life has been altered by both natural and manmade factors.

6. Substances released into the air today will _____ to ozone (臭氧) destruction well into the future.

7. Couples in strong marriages have a way of deescalating tension during _____ — they have a way of repairing.

8. There's a big difference between typing onto a screen and actually going out and _____ with people directly.

9. Consensus needs to be _____ about the need to implement a rapid shift towards a fair and ecologically sustainable economy.

10. In recent years, leaders from both parties have put forward _____ for increasing industrial energy efficiency.

11. Through such classics as *Singin' in the Rain*, Director Stanley Donen, a giant of the Hollywood musical, helped give us some of the most joyous sounds and _____ in movie history.

12. Make a(n) _____ goal each day, because if you show up at the gym without a plan, there's a good chance you'll walk on the treadmill (跑步机) for a half-hour and call it a day.

Exercise 2 Prefab Translation

I Discuss the meanings of the following prefabs in the text.

Prefabs

3	contribute to	23	a range of
5–6	resolve conflict	26	get sth. across to
6	make the most of	28	be aware of
19	a lack of	35–36	achieve the goal
19–20	common ground	56	make clear

II Translate the following into English, using the prefabs in the table above.

1 有助于自贸区的发展　_____

2 解决双方的重大利益冲突　_____

3 尽量利用好这一千载难逢的机会　_____

4 以勤补拙　_____

5 求同存异　_____

6 准备应付各种可能的情况　_____

7 设法让学生抓住教学要点　_____

8 充分意识到安全隐患　_____

9 用和平手段达到预期目的　_____

10 开宗明义　_____

B Partial Dictation

Listen to the following sentences once only and fill in the blanks with the exact words you hear.

1. Communication helps people _____, contribute to creative projects, make right decisions, and get ideas and proposals accepted.

2. Effective communication can _____ all the opportunities.

3. Every form of communication demands _____ another person or group of people—your audience.

4. A message _____ different codes by the sender through various communicative means.

5. It is very important for people to _____ their audience.

6. The content and the mode of communication should _____ satisfy the audience's needs.

7. Because the sender does not share _____ with the receiver, he or she should make sure that the message is as clear as possible.

8. It is essential to _____ the audience's broader multicultural context.

C Sentence Translation

Translate the Chinese sentences into English, using the expressions in the brackets.

1. 有人认为, 体育可以教会孩子们如何在课堂外与同伴打交道。(*interact with*)

2. 有些情况下, 感染过程可能会导致严重甚至致命的疾病。(*in some cases*)

3. 假如这个计划是可行的, 你们将如何启动实施呢?(*assuming that*)

4. 正因为如此, 这里的社会治安和社会风尚都很好。(*this is why*)

5. 在产品质量方面, 我们不能将就, 要精益求精。(*strive for*)

Translation Tips

Vivid Words, Big Thrills

One of the sentences in Para. 6 of the text reads: "You should <u>tailor</u> the content and the mode of communication to suit their features." Here, the underlined word "tailor" is used not as a noun for a dressmaker but as a verb, meaning making something fit for a specific purpose. The whole sentence can be translated into Chinese as "你应该依照他们的特性去匹配/调整沟通的内容和方式" or paraphrased into "交流内容和沟通方式要因人制宜".

The word "tailor", when used metaphorically, can bring a vivid effect to writing and translation alike. If you tailor something such as a plan to someone's needs, you make it suitable for a particular person or purpose by changing some minor details. Here are a few more examples to illustrate:

- We can <u>tailor</u> the program to the patient's needs. (我们可以根据病人的需要调整这个方案。)

- Exporters must <u>tailor</u> prices to the local market demand and the level of competition. (出口商必须根据当地的市场需求和竞争水平来调整价格。)

These examples show that to some extent, short but vivid words such as "tailor" do add amazingly expressive power to writing and translation.

Now, read and compare some groups of examples below, and note how small words can be used to achieve desired effect in the translation.

- Original sentence 1: 车祸中，女青年的左脚被死死地压在了货车的车轮底下。

  Draft translation: In the car accident, the left foot of the young girl <u>was caught firmly</u> beneath a wheel of the delivery van.

  Revised translation: In the car accident, the young girl's left foot <u>was pinned</u> beneath a wheel of the delivery van.

- Original sentence 2: 这件小事越闹越大，成了外交问题。

  Draft translation: This insignificant incident <u>became</u> a diplomatic issue.

  Revised translation: This insignificant incident <u>escalated/snowballed</u> into a diplomatic issue.

The revised versions above serve as living examples of dynamic thrills that vivid and pithy words may give to translation.

GRAMMARING

A introducing examples: *for example, such as…*

Examples make the writer's thoughts more concrete and comprehensible to the reader. To introduce an example, writers normally use the following expressions:

| for example | for instance | such as | e.g. |

1 *for example*

For example (for instance) can begin a new sentence. It can also appear within a sentence.

- When placed at the beginning of a sentence, *for example (for instance)* is followed by a comma (,). The clause before it may end with a full stop (.) or a semi-colon (;).
- When used as a mid-sentence comment, *for example (for instance)* is enclosed by commas.
- When *for example (for instance)* introduces a phrase or coordinated phrases as non-identifying details, a comma is placed before it.

See some examples:

At the Sentence Initial Position	Within a Sentence
■ Some inventions are useful. *For example*, the telephone allows people to communicate all over the world.	■ Offices can easily become more environmental-friendly by, *for example*, using recycled paper.
■ External noises are sights, sounds and other stimuli that draw people's attention away from the message. *For instance*, a pop-up advertisement may draw your attention away from a web page or blog.	■ A message is encoded by the sender through sounds, written words, images, video, spoken language or body language, *for example* gestures, facial expressions and tone of voice.
■ Bees communicate by dancing; *for example*, they do a kind of dance to tell other bees about the flowers.	■ The system will handle not only telephone calls and data messages but other signals that need high bandwidth, *for instance* those that encode TV pictures.

- There's no real difference between *for example* and *for instance*. *For instance* may be slightly more informal.
- The Latin abbreviation *e.g.* is mainly found in formal written texts. It is read aloud as "for example".

2 *such as*

We use *such as* to introduce an example or examples of something we mention. A comma is normally used before *such as* when we present a list of examples. See an example:

- The shop specializes in tropical fruits, *such as* pineapples, mangoes and papayas.

Commas are not used if the phrase of *such as* defines the word or words that precede it. See two examples:

- cultural factors *such as* values, beliefs and language
- Car companies *such as* Toyota and Ford manufacture their automobiles in many different countries around the world.

I Fill in the blanks with *such as* or *for example (for instance)*.

1. Some of the European languages come from Latin, _____ French, Italian and Spanish.

2. Hans hopes his research will help business companies work out the best ways for their employees to communicate. _____, the phone might be the best medium for selling their products where employees are encouraged to stretch the truth.

3. Ideas about polite behavior are different from one culture to another. Some societies, _____ America and Australia, are mobile and very open.

4. Countries _____ Sweden have a long record of welcoming refugees (难民) from all over the world.

5. This is why following a standard way to write a report, organize a meeting or give a presentation, _____, can facilitate communication.

6. Physical noise is interference in our environments, _____ noises made by others, overly dim or bright lights, spam and pop-up ads, extreme temperatures, and crowded conditions. Psychological noise refers to qualities in us that affect how we communicate and interpret others. _____, if you are preoccupied with a problem, you may be inattentive at a team meeting.

II Correct the mistakes in the use of connectors introducing examples in the following sentences.

1. There have been many leaders in history who have tried to rule the entire world. For instance, Julius Caesar and Alexander the Great.

   _____

2. It is communication skills, such as, writing, speaking and negotiating that are crucial to a life of success.

   _____

3. My friend loves going to restaurants which serve exotic foods, for example, last week he went to a restaurant which serves deep-fried rattlesnake.

   _____

4. He knows four languages, such as Chinese, English, Japanese and German.

   _____

5   Visual communication such as using pictures, graphs and the like, is fast gaining ground either to reinforce or to replace written messages.

6   He can play quite a few musical instruments. For example: he plays the flute, the guitar, and the piano.

7   Factors for instance nonverbal cues, the context and the people involved will heavily influence meaning.

B sentence connectors: *however, therefore*

1 *however*

We use *however* when we want to show that we are creating a contrast and introducing information which is unexpected or contradictory. *However* can be put in front, mid and end positions. For example:

- To be effective, your message must be clear. *However*, what is clear to you (the sender) may not be to the receiver, due to your different backgrounds.
- He had forgotten that there was a rainy season in the winter months. It was, *however*, a fine, soft rain and the air was warm.
- This transmission of messages is not always straightforward, *however*.

2 *therefore*

Therefore, which means "as a logical consequence", is used mostly in argumentation when one statement logically follows from another. It is common in scientific literature. For example:

- Assuming that they will share your views and your background knowledge may lead to misunderstandings; *therefore*, it is important to prepare thoroughly before communicating with people you have just met and who may be from a different context.
- The people involved need to work hard to build a mutual understanding and, *therefore*, exchange several messages or use a range of different media.

> Note the use of punctuation marks:
>
> ☑ There is still much to discuss. *Therefore*(,) we shall return to this item at our next meeting.
>
> ☑ There is still much to discuss; *therefore*(,) we shall return to this item at our next meeting.
>
> ☑ There is still much to discuss, and(,) *therefore*(,) we shall return to this item at our next meeting.
>
> ☒ There is still much to discuss, *therefore* we shall return to this item at our next meeting.

I Fill in the blanks with *therefore* or *however*.

1   Our lives have become too complicated; _____, we've decided to simplify things and move to the country.

2   I feel a bit tired. _____, it's probably just the weather.

3   Effective communication is heavily dependent on effective listening; _____, most conversations do not take place with the full attention of those taking part.

4   This sentence isn't giving any detailed information. _____, it isn't necessary.

5   People do not read business memoranda for the pleasure of reading. _____, highly literary prose is not desirable in business writing.

6   Studies have shown that listening is the most frequent aspect of workplace communication. _____, research suggests that people generally achieve no more than 25%–50% accuracy in interpreting the meaning of each other's remarks.

II Improve the paragraphs by adding appropriate sentence connectors.

1   Language may act as a barrier to communication. _____, even when communicating in the same language, the terminology used in a message may act as a barrier if it is not fully understood by the receiver. _____, a message that includes a lot of specialist jargon and abbreviations will not be understood by a receiver who is not familiar with the terminology used.

2   Active listening is a skill that can be acquired and developed with practice. _____, this skill can be difficult to master and will, _____, take time and patience. As well as giving full attention to the speaker, it is important that the "active listener" is also "seen" to be listening. By providing this "feedback" the person speaking will usually feel more at ease and, _____, communicate more easily, openly and honestly.

3   Nonverbal communication has been said to have a greater universality than language. _____, nonverbal cues can also differ dramatically from culture to culture. An American hand gesture meaning "OK", _____, would be viewed as obscene in some South American countries.

COMMUNICATING

A Viewing: Business Communication

I　Get Prepared: Read the passage and fill in the blanks with the words or phrase from the box.

> intent　　frustrated　　nonverbal　　build up　　generalization　　counter

Strategies for Improving Communication

There are four ways you can use to improve your communication. First, use as many levels of communication as possible. In addition to verbal language (both written and spoken), proper use of (1) _____ language like body language is expected in communication as well. Second, clearly share your (2) _____ for the communication. If you state your goal, you increase the chances that the receiver will hear it. Third, avoid over (3) _____. Exaggerating expressions and strong statements like "You always…" or "You never…" give the other person a place to (4) _____ you with examples. Last, speak for yourself. Use something called "I" statements. For instance, instead of saying "It annoys everyone when you are late for meetings," say something like "When you are late for meetings, I feel (5) _____ because I have to rework the agenda." These four tips are highly recommended as they can help you cut down the situations that could (6) _____ to difficult conversations.

II　Get Prepared: You will hear these words and expressions in the video. Read them aloud.

Words and Expressions	
hear back from	收到回复
fall into the trap	掉进陷阱，陷入误区
speed up	加速
slow down	减慢
switch	调换，变化
poke one's head into	搜寻，查找
top of mind	要紧事
add-on	插件，附加组件

III Watch and Listen for Gist: Watch the video and complete the sentences. ▶ 2.03

The speaker mainly talks about how to (1) _____ while (2) _____. The solutions he provides are setting (3) _____ and managing (4) _____.

IV Watch and Listen for Details: Watch ▶ 2.03 again and decide whether the following statements are true (T) or false (F). Then correct the false statements.

1 When you're anxiously waiting for a reply from someone, you may feel annoyed if you do not receive any response from him or her. T F

2 According to the speaker, scheduled emails should only be used for urgent situations. T F

3 The speaker suggests that you reply in five minutes when you receive emails about unimportant things. T F

4 If you reply immediately to an email about something not urgent, the receiver of your message would think that you like to receive more of such emails. T F

5 You do not have to reply quickly to an email even if it is important. T F

6 Outlook is the only email app you can use to delay sending an email. T F

V Watch and Infer Information: Watch part of the video and answer the question. ▶ 2.04

What does the speaker mean when he says "Past patterns of communication will indicate future likelihood of communication."?

What the speaker intends to say is that _____

_____

_____

_____

_____

Unit 2 **Communication** 47

VI Watch and Listen for Language Use: Watch part of the video and fill in the blanks with the exact words you hear.

First, if you're going to be working on an urgent project with a team member and you're (1) _____ a deadline, (2) _____ just two minutes to set expectations for response rates. Something like this: We've got a deadline fast approaching on Tuesday. Because of that, I think both of us should be more responsive on email for the next few days. Let's try to check our email (3) _____ and (4) _____ each other whenever we see a message.

But (5) _____ you (6) _____ the email, checked it, and you saw something you want to deal with because it's (7) _____?

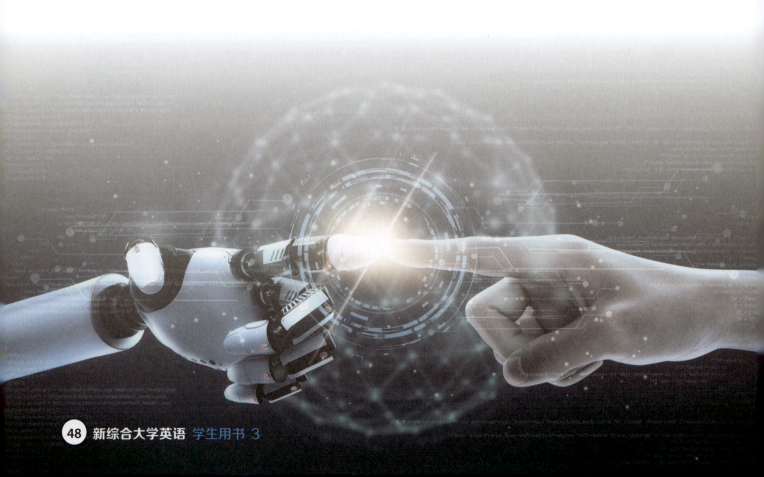

B Speaking

Activity 1 Body Language

I Complete the speech by filling in the blanks with appropriate expressions. Then listen and check your answers.

🎧 2.06

Body language is a part of (1) _____ language. It includes things like stance, gestures, facial expressions, and even small things that are barely perceptible like a brief (2) _____ of the shoulder or nod of the head.

(3) _____ is a key element of nonverbal contact in much of the Western world. (4) _____ look someone in the eyes enough but not too much if you want to indicate that you're direct and forthright. Evading eye contact may (5) _____ you're shy or being deceptive, or alternately, it can (6) _____ annoyance or disgust with someone.

How we gesture can (7) _____ people the level of confidence we have, or if we're a little too emphatic in our opinions. Huge gestures may (8) _____ we have something to prove. Moderate gesturing may simply (9) _____ we're engaged and confident in what we have to say.

Even the way you turn your head, shrug, yawn, look at your watch may all be forms of nonverbal communication that (10) _____ clear signals to other people. (11) _____, never look at your watch or the clock above your head when you're in a meeting with your boss. It can send the message that you're (12) _____, which isn't a positive message to send.

It would be impossible to describe all the ways we use nonverbal language, but it's important to remember that nonverbal language isn't (13) _____ universal. If you're observing body movements that seem (14) _____, consider cultural or regional differences that may (15) _____ it.

II Pair Work: Practice the speech in front of your partner.

III Read the useful expressions aloud.

Useful Expressions for Delivering Information	
■ to send clear signals to…	■ It may say/mean/suggest that…
■ to get a message across to…	■ That can convey something.
■ It helps to…	■ This can tell us something.

Unit 2 **Communication** 49

IV Pair Work: What do you know about the following body language? Take turns asking and answering the question with a partner. Add more gestures and check whether your partner knows their meanings. Then summarize what body language delivers negative information, and what sends positive signals.

> What body language do you like to use when communicating with others?

> I'd like to keep eye contact with them to say I'm listening.

> I do that too. I also nod my head. What do you do when you get bored?

> Well, I simply change the topic.

Activity 2   How to Be an Active Listener?

I Read the information about strategies to be an active listener. Add more strategies that you prefer to use.

Strategies to Be an Active Listener in Communication
Use nonverbal language to send signals to speakers that you are listening. For example, you can nod your head to show agreement or lean forward to show interest.
Ask questions. When you're the receiver, your goal is to make sure you're hearing the message accurately. If something is not clear, ask a question that will provide clarity.
Confirm what you understand. Share back to the person what you think he or she said by paraphrasing his or her words so that you can check whether you have got the message correctly.
Share your perspective. Once the other person feels heard, you can share what you think and feel. Be as clear as possible. Identify where you're in agreement and where you disagree. If the situation's complex, take each piece separately.
More: _____

II **Group Work:** Use the information in the chart above and discuss with your partners how to be an active listener in communication. You may use the model dialog for help.

A: Do you enjoy communicating with others?

B: No, definitely not. I don't think I'm sociable. Actually, I'd rather put my nose down to endless paperwork than deal with people.

C: Neither do I. I find it hard to keep talking on one topic.

B: I'd rather turn myself to be a listener. If I'm interested in the topic, I'd use body language to encourage the speaker to say more about it.

C: What body language?

B: Usually, I just nod my head.

C: Do you have any suggestions on how to change the subject of a conversation? I feel so frustrated when someone keeps talking nonsense.

A: Do not fall into the trap of thinking that interrupting or even stopping others' talking is impolite. On many occasions, we just have to do that for our own benefit.

B: Little eye contact with the speaker and tense facial expressions are good body language to use to tell others that you are bored.

Unit 2 **Communication**

C Writing

I Fill in the blanks with phrases from the box to complete the paragraph. You may need to make necessary changes to some of the phrases.

build an effective / a good relationship with	innovative projects
interact with	resolve conflict
body language	facial expressions
common ground	build a mutual understanding
mode of communication	a range of
achieve one's goal/purpose	be mindful of
in some cases	

Effective communication is essential for business. How to (1) _____ others in a proper way is often deemed as a kind of art. Firstly, we need to seek (2) _____. To a considerable extent our smooth communication depends on our shared knowledge. Secondly, ways of communication are many and varied. When we choose the (3) _____ _____, we should (4) _____ what might turn out to be obstacles. We may use (5) _____ or (6) _____ to convey our messages. Of course, we may have vastly different views or even opposing opinions (7) _____. When that happens, we need sufficient patience and wisdom to (8) _____. Thirdly, if we wish to keep the communication line open, it is equally important for us to (9) _____ each other. A good relationship is a long-term guarantee for effective communication to (10) _____.

II Now write an essay of about 220 words on *Business Communication*. You may use the phrases from the box above.

TEXT B — The Long-term Career Damage from Not Talking to Your Kids About Money

Richard Harris

As I travel across the country and around the world training salespeople at all kinds of businesses, I've learned to **spot** those who grew up in homes in which money was rarely, if ever, discussed. They're often the ones struggling the most in the world of work.

Fellow parents: I know it can be uncomfortable and awkward. But if you don't talk to your kids about money, you could be causing long-term damage, **impeding** their future careers.

This is true for any field. To succeed, you have to be able to **navigate** conversations, and, in many cases negotiate. That requires talking about money.

And while about 14.5 million Americans have sales related jobs, just about everyone has to sell. In interviews, you "sell" yourself for jobs and promotions. As an employee or **entrepreneur**, you "sell" your ideas to build support. And as more Americans become **freelancers**—they may be the majority within a decade—people constantly have to sell themselves as candidates for **gig** work.

Most buyers and hiring managers want, and appreciate, straightforward communication. They're looking for the value **proposition**. How much good will this do for them? What's the economic impact?

I see people **choke up** all the time when it comes to answering these questions. They're also afraid to ask questions, like, "What's your budget?" Or, "What's the salary range?"

It's very simple: The people who are comfortable having

spot *vt.* 看见，注意到

impede *vt.* 妨碍

navigate *vt.* 驾驭

entrepreneur *n.* 企业家

freelancer *n.* 自由职业者
gig *n.* 零工

proposition *n.* 提议，主张

choke up 噎住，说不出话来

these conversations make better deals, and more of them. The people who aren't comfortable talking about money end up losing opportunities.

Lots of experts call on parents to talk about money at home, and offer guidance on which financial topics kids are ready to learn at different ages. But in many families the topic remains **taboo**.

A study from Chase Slate found that a little more than half (56 percent) of parents have discussed money with their kids. T. Rowe Price, meanwhile, found that 77 percent of parents at least touch on "**monetary** requirements" as part of discussions about future careers, and 73 percent believe "it's important to include kids in discussions regarding the family finances". But 41 percent admitted they sometimes avoid talking to their kids about money.

Some people have a sense of shame around finance. And some were taught things like "never count someone else's money"—an **adage** that can lead to good lessons like not feeling jealous of another person, but can also lead people to believe it's bad to even bring up money.

I've had trainees tell me they hear **nagging** voices of their parents in their heads saying, "Don't ask about that!"

I have to explain to them that it's not rude to discuss money, particularly with someone considering buying what you offer. And I know from experience that learning from your parents about the family budget and specific aspects of the economy can be very helpful.

My parents were open about money. They taught me about stocks when I was 6. I started buying stocks at age 15.

Now, my wife and I pass these lessons on to our boys, ages 10 and 9. Our conversations run the **gamut**. We talk about budgeting; how my business works; how people can get better at making money; **real estate**, and more. Like 69 percent of parents in the T. Rowe Price survey, we open up to our kids about financial mistakes we've made.

When we go grocery shopping, we each guess the total bill. It's fun, but also draws attention to the costs, emphasizing that food doesn't just magically appear in the house. And we've taken our kids to the bank to help them set up their own savings accounts.

We've also helped them make **lemonade** stands, and have

taught them to always give a **portion** of profits to charity. It's fantastic to watch your kids walk up to the local **firehouse**, hand over a contribution and explain how they made the money—and to see the mix of joy and confusion on the firefighters' faces.

Of course, kids don't just learn from what parents tell them. They learn more from what we do. So it's important that we walk the walk. (More than 80 percent of parents surveyed by T. Rowe Price believe they set a good example with money, but 40 percent still admit that they take a "Do as I say, not as I do" attitude in talking to kids about money.)

It's also true that kids can, and should, learn about financial issues and topics in other ways, including in school. But the role of parents is tough to overestimate. As the Chase study put it, "Americans say they owe their financial foundation to their parents." The question is whether it will be a solid enough foundation for them to face the future.

portion *n.* 部分
firehouse *n.* 消防站

Notes

1. **Richard Harris**
   Richard Harris, CEO of The Harris Consulting Group, is one of the most influential sales leaders in the software industry with clients such as Google, VISA, and SalesLoft. He is also the current Director of Sales Consulting and Training for Sales Hacker.

2. **Chase (Line 35)**
   Chase can be traced back to the 18th century and was founded under the name of the Bank of the Manhattan Company. Nowadays it serves as the U.S. consumer and commercial banking business of JP Morgan Chase & Co., a leading global financial services firm.

3. **T. Rowe Price (Lines 36–37)**
   Thomas Rowe Price, Jr. (1898–1983) was an American investment banker and businessman. He was the founder of T. Rowe Price, an American publicly owned investment firm established in 1937 and headquartered in Baltimore.

EXERCISES

A Reading for Gist

Answer the following questions according to your understanding of Text B.

1. What are the benefits of talking about money with kids?

   _____

   _____

2. What is the attitude of the author's family towards finances?

   _____

   _____

B Reading for Details

Each of the following statements contains information given in the text. Identify and write down the corresponding number of the paragraph from which the information is derived.

1. It is beneficial to let children know about their family budget.   Para. _____

2. People who had little opportunity to talk about money in their childhood are struggling the most to earn their living.   Para. _____

3. The role of parents about financial issues towards children cannot be overemphasized.   Para. _____

4. Financial mistakes should also be open to kids.   Para. _____

5. Forty-one percent of parents sometimes feel unwilling to discuss money with their kids according to T. Rowe Price.   Para. _____

6. The author and his wife have taught kids how to get involved in the charity.   Para. _____

C Reading Beyond

Discuss with your group members the following topic for about 15 minutes. Then share your opinions with the whole class.

Topic: What was your parents' attitude towards talking about money when you were young?

D Prefabs

Write the Chinese meanings of the following prefabs in the text.

the world of work　　　　　　　　　　_____

in many cases　　　　　　　　　　　 _____

when it comes to doing　　　　　　　 _____

end up doing　　　　　　　　　　　 _____

a sense of shame　　　　　　　　　　_____

be open about　　　　　　　　　　　_____

walk the walk　　　　　　　　　　　_____

cause damage　　　　　　　　　　　 _____

build support　　　　　　　　　　　 _____

make deals　　　　　　　　　　　　 _____

touch on sth.　　　　　　　　　　　 _____

feel jealous of　　　　　　　　　　　 _____

open up to sb.　　　　　　　　　　　_____

as... put it　　　　　　　　　　　　 _____

E Sentence Translation

I Translate the English sentences into Chinese.

1. As I travel across the country and around the world training salespeople at all kinds of businesses, I've learned to spot those who grew up in homes in which money was rarely, if ever, discussed.

2. Lots of experts call on parents to talk about money at home, and offer guidance on which financial topics kids are ready to learn at different ages. But in many families the topic remains taboo.

3. It's fantastic to watch your kids walk up to the local firehouse, hand over a contribution and explain how they made the money—and to see the mix of joy and confusion on the firefighters' faces.

II Translate the Chinese sentences into English, using the expressions in the brackets.

1. 这个问题令他哽咽无语。(choke up)

2. 每次他们去跳舞，总是扫兴而归。(end up)

3. 媒体经常能够通过新闻报道引起公众注意来帮助解决问题。(draw attention to)

Unit 3 Volunteering

Warming Up

Memorize and comment on the following quotations on life.

1. 人的生命是有限的,可是,为人民服务是无限的,我要把有限的生命,投入到无限的为人民服务之中去。

   ——雷锋

2. We make a living by what we get, but we make a life by what we give.

   — Winston Churchill

INITIAL READING

A Vocabulary

Read the new words aloud and figure out their meanings in the text.

New Words

20 **intrinsic** /ɪnˈtrɪnzɪk/ adj.

25 **simplistic** /sɪmˈplɪstɪk/ adj.

28 **slippery** /ˈslɪpəri/ adj.

28 **slope** /sləʊp/ n.

30 **volunteerism** /ˌvɒlənˈtɪərɪzəm/ n.

31 **vibrant** /ˈvaɪbrənt/ adj.

32 **reliant** /rɪˈlaɪənt/ adj.

36 **petroleum** /pəˈtrəʊliəm/ n.

39 **hospice** /ˈhɒspɪs/ n.

39 **spontaneous** /spɒnˈteɪniəs/ adj.

40 **shovel** /ˈʃʌvəl/ vt.

40 **strand** /strænd/ vt.

41 **bind** /baɪnd/ vt.

45 **insidiously** /ɪnˈsɪdiəsli/ adv.

45 **mandatory** /ˈmændətəri/ adj.

B Skimming

Read Text A and go through the statements within eight minutes. Circle the numbers of the correct statements.

1   This text is about the real meaning of volunteering.

2   "Count" is used twice in Einstein's quote with the same meaning.

3   Not everyone believes that volunteering is all about money.

4   The author puts forward many questions in Para. 2 without giving any definite answers.

5   Networking is one of the motives for people to be volunteers.

6   One may feel good about himself while volunteering.

7   According to the author, the practice of calculating the total voluntary time demonstrates the deficiencies in measuring volunteering by money.

8   Helping people in big events is more meaningful than helping one's neighbors.

9   It is beneficial to measure the value of volunteering by money.

10 The author believes the longer time people spend on voluntary work, the better they are.

TEXT A The Value of Volunteering

Arden Brummell

"Not everything that counts can be counted. And not everything that can be counted counts."—Albert Einstein

In 1988, a French observer to the Calgary Olympics was impressed with the huge effort, commitment and contribution of volunteers to the games. He said the 1992 Albertville games would also use volunteers. How would he recruit them, he was asked. "We'll pay them," he said.

What is a volunteer? What is the value of volunteering? Is volunteering about money? Should we measure it that way? Most people would say no. Volunteering is not about money. Volunteering is about giving, contributing, and helping other individuals and the community at large. It is working with others to make a meaningful contribution to a better community.

People volunteer for an endless variety of reasons. Many people want to gain experience, acquire new skills, meet new people, or expand their network of contacts as a way to get a new job or start a career. Others just want to give back to their community, to help a friend or promote a worthwhile activity. They do it because it makes them feel good. It gives them what current Chair of Volunteer Calgary, Dan O'Grady describes as a "private smile".

This is the **intrinsic** value of volunteering. It is not about money. And volunteering should not be measured that way. Ever. We can add up the hours but not a dollar value. Others would like to do so. The federal government, for example, would like to add up the billions of hours of volunteer time in Canada, multiply by an hourly rate and determine the economic value of volunteering. This is **simplistic** and dangerous. First, it assumes that only economic measurements are valuable and second, that volunteer time is free labour.

This is a **slippery slope**. It infers that volunteer work is replacing paid labour. It infers that if work is not paid for, it is not valuable. It reduces **volunteerism** to hours worked instead of contribution made. It ignores the value of volunteers in creating a **vibrant** civil society—dynamic, engaged and self-**reliant**.

To attempt to put a dollar figure on the value of volunteerism cheapens and undermines the basic concept. Volunteering is rich and diverse. Volunteering is not just about organizing hundreds or thousands of volunteers for large events like the Olympics, the World **Petroleum**

Congress or the Stampede, of which Calgary is justly proud. It is thousands of volunteers in minor league sports, shelters for the homeless, giving aid to seniors, holding hands in a **hospice** or cleaning up a local stream bed. It is **spontaneous** acts of kindness like helping a neighbour **shovel** their walk, coming to the aid of a **stranded** motorist or helping an elderly person cross a busy street. These large and small acts, given freely, are what **bind** communities together. Volunteering is helping, not hiring; giving, not taking; contributing, not counting.

Some believe putting a dollar amount on volunteering does no harm. This is wrong. It **insidiously** undermines the true value of volunteerism. Like the term "**mandatory** volunteerism", it distorts the meaning and spirit of volunteering. We want motivated, not mandatory volunteers. We want willing, not "paid" volunteers.

Add up the hours if you must but do not be blinded by the numbers. The value of volunteering is much deeper, much more fulfilling and much more important in contributing to a healthy and vibrant community than money can ever measure.

In the end, we cannot and should not put a dollar value on volunteering. How can we put a monetary value on ordinary people doing extraordinary things?

Notes

1. **Arden Brummell**

   Arden Brummell's particular focus is on scenario planning facilitation to promote organizational learning and strategic business development. He is a former Director of The Strategic Leadership Forum, a member of The World Future Society, past Chair of Volunteer Calgary and Leadership Calgary.

2. **the Olympics (Line 3)**

   The Olympics are the world's premier international sporting event, featuring thousands of athletes from around the world, and affecting global commerce, politics and diplomacy. They are currently held biennially, with Summer and Winter Olympic Games alternating. The Olympic symbol, known as the Olympic rings, consists of five intertwined rings and represents the unity of the five inhabited continents. The motto is "Citius, Altius, Fortius—Communis", a Latin expression meaning "Faster, Higher, Stronger—Together".

3. **the Calgary Olympics (Line 3)**

   Calgary 1988 Olympic Winter Games, officially known as the XV Olympic Winter Games and commonly known as Calgary '88, were a multi-sport event held from February 13 to 28, 1988, in Calgary, Alberta, Canada. It was the first Winter Olympic Games to be held for 16 days, like the counterpart Summer Olympic Games.

4. **volunteering (Line 7)**

   Volunteering is a voluntary act of an

individual or a group freely giving time and labor for community service. Many volunteers are specifically trained in the areas where they work, such as medicine, education, or emergency rescue. Others serve on an as-needed basis, such as in response to a natural disaster.

5. **the World Petroleum Congress (Lines 36–37)**
The World Petroleum Congress is an oil and gas industry forum and international organization representing the petroleum sector worldwide. Every three years, it organizes a global discussion of oil and gas issues.

STUDY READING

A Structure Analysis

Fill in each blank with no more than four words according to your understanding of the structure and content of the text.

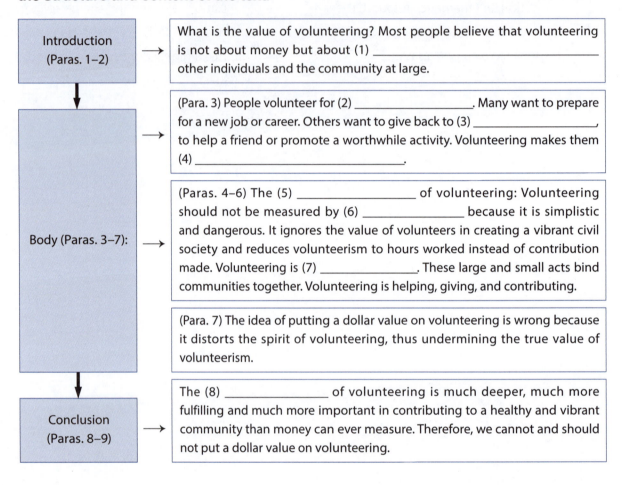

Introduction (Paras. 1–2) →	What is the value of volunteering? Most people believe that volunteering is not about money but about (1) _____ other individuals and the community at large.
Body (Paras. 3–7): →	(Para. 3) People volunteer for (2) _____. Many want to prepare for a new job or career. Others want to give back to (3) _____, to help a friend or promote a worthwhile activity. Volunteering makes them (4) _____.
→	(Paras. 4–6) The (5) _____ of volunteering: Volunteering should not be measured by (6) _____ because it is simplistic and dangerous. It ignores the value of volunteers in creating a vibrant civil society and reduces volunteerism to hours worked instead of contribution made. Volunteering is (7) _____. These large and small acts bind communities together. Volunteering is helping, giving, and contributing.
→	(Para. 7) The idea of putting a dollar value on volunteering is wrong because it distorts the spirit of volunteering, thus undermining the true value of volunteerism.
Conclusion (Paras. 8–9) →	The (8) _____ of volunteering is much deeper, much more fulfilling and much more important in contributing to a healthy and vibrant community than money can ever measure. Therefore, we cannot and should not put a dollar value on volunteering.

B Reading Comprehension

I Sequencing: Identify the order of the following statements according to the text.

_____ A Volunteers are to create a vibrant civil society, which is ignored by some people.

_____ B Accompanying the old at the end of their lives is a kind of volunteer work.

_____ C Most people believe that volunteering should not be measured in terms of money.

_____ D The value of volunteering is too deep and too important to be measured by money.

_____ E To socialize with more people is one of the reasons for some people to volunteer.

_____ F It is dangerous for the federal government to do statistical analysis of the volunteer work.

II Blank Filling: Fill in each blank with no more than three words based on the text.

1. In the 1988 Olympic Games, a Frenchman _____ the huge endeavor, commitment and contribution of volunteers.

2. Volunteering is not about money but about giving, contributing, and helping others and the community _____.

3. There are _____ reasons for people to do volunteer work.

4. Some volunteers just want to _____ their community because this will give them a "private smile".

5. The intrinsic value of volunteering should not _____ money.

6. Some believe that we cannot put a dollar value on volunteering but can _____ the hours of volunteer time.

7. The acts of volunteering, no matter big or small, _____, tend to unite communities together.

8. From the perspective of _____ a healthy and vigorous community, the value of volunteering is much more meaningful and significant than money can measure.

III Group Work: Have you ever volunteered? Work in groups and have a discussion on what you can learn from volunteering based on your own experience, and then give a presentation in front of the whole class.

WORD BUILDING

A Prefabs

Exercise 1   Blank Filling: Active Words

I Study the meanings of the active nouns, verbs and adjectives in the table.

Active Words

4	**commitment** /kə'mɪtmənt/ *n.* N *to* n	[U] Commitment is a strong belief in an idea or system. *commitment to his ideals*
6	**recruit** /rɪ'kruːt/ *vt.* V n	If you recruit people for an organization, you select them and persuade them to join it or work for it. *to recruit students to the Student Union*
10	**individual** /ˌɪndɪ'vɪdʒuəl/ *n.*	[C] An individual is a person. *anonymous individuals*
10	**community** /kə'mjuːnəti/ *n.*	[U] A particular community is a group of people who are similar in some way. *language community*
14	**acquire** /ə'kwaɪə(r)/ *vt.* V n	If you acquire something such as a skill or a habit, you learn it, or develop it through your daily life or experience. *to acquire knowledge*
14	**expand** /ɪk'spænd/ *vt.* V n	If something such as a business, organization, or service expands, or if you expand it, it becomes bigger and includes more people, goods, or activities. *to expand the ceramics industry*
15	**contact** /'kɒntækt/ *n.*	[C] A contact is someone you know in an organization or profession who helps you or gives you information.
16	**promote** /prə'məʊt/ *vt.* V n	If people promote something, they help or encourage it to happen, increase, or spread. *to promote economic growth*
18	**current** /'kʌrənt/ *adj.*	Current means happening, being used, or being done at the present time. *the current situation*
30	**ignore** /ɪg'nɔː(r)/ *vt.* V n	If you ignore someone or something, you pay no attention to them. *to ignore the problem*
31	**dynamic** /daɪ'næmɪk/ *adj.*	If you describe something as dynamic, you approve of it because it is very active and energetic. *the most dynamic economic region in the world*
34	**undermine** /ˌʌndə'maɪn/ *vt.* V n	If you undermine something such as a feeling or a system, you make it less strong or less secure than it was before, often by a gradual process or by repeated efforts. *to undermine one's feeling of being adult*
35	**diverse** /daɪ'vɜːs/ *adj.*	If a group of things is diverse, it is made up of a wide variety of things. *a very diverse city*
46	**distort** /dɪ'stɔːt/ *vt.* V n	If you distort a statement, fact, or idea, you report or represent it in an untrue way. *to distort reality*

II **Now complete the sentences with the words in the table above. You need to change the form where necessary.**

1 I've worked seventeen years for this company in a variety of roles and made a huge _____ to the organization.

2 Common languages, religions, and technologies may bind _____ together while their absence may keep them apart.

3 Since the encyclopedia covers many issues with distinct disciplinary emphases, in the search for authors I was called upon to expand my network of _____ of academics and activists in the social sciences.

4 It might seem reasonable to think so, but if we look at the _____ situation, it seems to us that there is a large amount of uncertainty—but little risk.

5 There are great _____ differences within and between the two languages of bilingual children and current assessment instruments are not designed to differentiate differences from true disabilities in these children.

6 Together government and the private sector can work to produce a vibrant, _____ economy that offers its people the greatest possible opportunity to satisfy their wants and needs.

7 Consideration of gender and diversity is also important to ensure the texts are appealing to both male and female students and to provide an opportunity for students to learn about _____ cultures in the classroom.

8 When children go to camp, they learn to be more independent and _____ social skills.

9 International Association for Volunteer Effort is an association of individuals who work to _____ volunteerism in countries throughout the world.

10 Some believe that banning cellphones and personal electronic devices in schools _____ the value of technology in today's education.

11 It is beneficial to structure activities so that youth with disabilities become well known to other participants and thus _____ their networks of support.

12 The lawyer was accused of _____ the meaning of some concepts in this case.

13 Volunteers _____ from local government, organizations, and businesses to monitor ozone sampling stations and collect samples.

14 High divorce rates and out-of-wedlock (婚外的) births, many believe, have _____ the concept of the family and robbed large numbers of children of the support, security and stability they deserve.

Unit 3 **Volunteering**

Exercise 2 Prefab Translation

I Discuss the meanings of the following prefabs in the text.

Prefabs

8	that way	15	start a career
10	at large	37	be proud of
11	work with	37	hold hands
14	gain experience	38	give aid to
15	network of contacts	41–42	bind together

II Translate the following into English, using the prefabs in the table above.

1. 出于礼貌才这么说的 _____
2. 颇受广大英语读者的欢迎 _____
3. 一个很好共事的人 _____
4. 保持与社会各界的广泛联系 _____
5. 从实践中获取宝贵的经验 _____
6. 成家立业 _____
7. 为美丽的家乡感到无比自豪 _____
8. 推进边远地区的扶贫工程 _____
9. 携手共创健康美好的未来 _____
10. 将箱子等行李捆在一起 _____

B Partial Dictation

Listen to the following sentences once only and fill in the blanks with the exact words you hear.

1 The volunteers' great effort, _____ left a deep impression on the audience.

2 Volunteering has an important attribute that can _____ a better community.

3 The intrinsic value of volunteering does not _____ economic worth.

4 It is _____ that volunteering work is determined by economic measurements.

5 Volunteering can help to create a society that is full of _____.

6 Both large and small volunteering acts are helpful _____ better communities.

7 Self-motivated and _____ is what we really want.

8 People can add up the hours of volunteering work, but should not _____ the numbers.

C Sentence Translation

Translate the Chinese sentences into English, using the expressions in the brackets.

1 他的诚恳直率给我们留下了很深刻的印象。(*be impressed by*)

_____

2 我们认为这是一个关乎世界和平和人类进步的重大事件。(*be about*)

_____

3 不要开会时赞成，会后又反悔说不赞成。(*say no*)

_____

4 绿色是一种快乐的颜色，让我们感到生活无比美好。(*feel good*)

_____

5 做完饭菜后，一定要把厨房收拾干净。(*clean up*)

_____

Translation Tips

"Hospice" and Its Corresponding Expressions in Chinese

Volunteering, the main theme of the text, is defined in the middle of Para. 6 as "It is thousands of volunteers in minor league sports, shelters for the homeless, giving aid to seniors, holding hands in a hospice or cleaning up a local stream bed." The underlined word "hospice" might be a new word. According to dictionaries, a hospice is a special hospital for people who are dying, where their practical and emotional needs are dealt with as well as their medical needs.

Can you suggest a proper Chinese translation for "hospice"?

Yes, one of its counterparts in Chinese is "临终关怀医院". Other corresponding expressions are "安宁疗护中心" or "安养院", somewhat tongue-twisting but currently gaining media exposure from time to time.

In the same manner, "hospice care" can be translated into Chinese as "临终关怀", "安宁疗护" or "安养关怀", which attends to the physical, emotional and sometimes spiritual needs of the terminally ill or elderly patients. And what the hospice doctors and nurses (临终关怀医护人员) do is to ease the pain and symptoms of the patients and help them die with more comfort and dignity.

GRAMMARING

A articles: *a, an, the*

Articles are words that come before nouns and define them as specific or unspecific.

To talk about things or people in general, we usually use

φ + plural noun	■ φ *People* volunteer for an endless variety of reasons.
φ + uncountable noun	■ Volunteering is not about φ *money*.
a/an + singular noun	■ Many people want to gain experience as a way to get *a new job* or start *a career*.
the + singular noun (usually when we are talking about science and technology)	■ Galileo claimed that he had invented *the telescope*.

To talk about particular things or people, we use

a/an + singular noun (indefinite reference) • when we mention something for the first time.	■ A French observer to *the* Calgary Olympics was impressed with *the* huge effort, commitment and contribution of volunteers to *the* games. ■ She stopped and lit *a* match. The wind almost blew out *the* flame. ■ What is *the* President doing about all this?
the + noun (definite reference) • when identity has been established by an earlier mention; • when identity is established by the postmodification that follows the noun; • when the object is the only one that exists or has existed; • when reference is made to a specific place or organization.	

We use "*the* + adjective" to talk about groups of people. For example:

■ It shelters for *the homeless* and gives aid to seniors.

I   Put the articles *a/an* or *the* in the blanks, or φ if no article is necessary.

1   It ignores _____ value of volunteers in creating _____ vibrant civil society.

2   Babies need _____ comfort of their mother's arms.

3   _____ computer can only do what you program it to do.

4   The pension crisis will never be solved if _____ young are not working and _____ economy is not growing.

5   _____ general education is perhaps more important than _____ exact knowledge of some particular theory.

6   Volunteering is working with _____ others to make _____ meaningful contribution to _____ better community.

Unit 3 **Volunteering**

7   If you're considering _____ new career, volunteering can help you get experience in your area of interest and meet people in _____ field. Even if you're not planning on changing _____ careers, volunteering gives you _____ opportunity to practice _____ important skills used in _____ workplace, such as teamwork, communication, problem solving, project planning, task management, and organization.

8   One of the benefits of volunteering is _____ impact on _____ community. Volunteering allows you to connect to your community and make it _____ better place. Even helping out with _____ smallest tasks can make _____ real difference to _____ lives of people, animals, and organizations in need. And volunteering is _____ two-way street: It can benefit you and your family as much as _____ cause you choose to help. Dedicating your time as _____ volunteer helps you make _____ new friends, expand your network, and boost your social skills.

II Correct the mistakes in the use of articles in the following text.

Two weeks I spent volunteering in Morocco, Rabat, were unimaginable. I not only fell in love with Morocco, but also an volunteering, traveling, teaching and experience of new culture. Upon arrival in Rabat, a buzzing, thrilling and exciting atmosphere of Medina immediately engaged me. It was huge area of various windy roads with the tall but small houses.

B sentence connectors: listing (*first, second, ...*)

In formal writing and speech, we indicate the order of things in a sequence by using the following sentence connectors:

first(ly)	second(ly)	third(ly)	for a start
first of all	to begin with	to start with	in the first place
for another thing	then	next	lastly
in conclusion	to sum up	finally	

See two examples:

- *First*, it assumes that only economic measurements are valuable and *second*, that volunteer time is free labor.

- What are the advantages of geothermal energy? *Firstly*, there's no fuel required; the energy already exists. *Secondly*, there's plenty of it. *Finally*, I want to say something about the heat pump.

Firstly may appear more formal than *first* and is often recommended for the formal enumeration of arguments. Yet many writers prefer *first*, even when the remaining items or points are introduced with *secondly, thirdly*, etc.

I Add connectors to the following paragraphs.

1. Volunteer work improves your job prospects for two main reasons. _____, in a competitive job market, professional networking is essential and volunteering is a fantastic way of expanding yours. Getting a professional recommendation from someone can significantly increase your chances of getting a job. _____, employers look favorably on job applicants who have volunteer work on their resume. It makes a very positive impression.

2. There are three reasons why I don't want to hire him. _____, he doesn't have the required qualifications. _____, he lacks work experience. And _____, he is not strong enough for the job.

II Complete the following passage by listing at least three benefits of volunteering. Use the appropriate sentence connectors.

Volunteering offers vital help to people in need, but the benefits can be even greater for you, the volunteer. _____

_____
_____
_____
_____
_____

C prepositions: *for, of, to*

1 *for*

We use the preposition *for* before a noun or a noun phrase to

- talk about reason or purpose;
- say how long an action or a situation lasts.

See three examples:

- I went to the college *for* an interview with Professor Willis.
- People volunteer *for* an endless variety of reasons.
- He will be away *for* the next few days.

2 *of*

We use the preposition *of* to

- express the relationship between a part and a whole;
- indicate an association between two entities;

- say what sb. /sth. is, consists of, or contains.

See two examples:

- Group activities expand one's network *of* contacts.
- Emily and her friends went to the aid *of* a stranger who is being bullied by a gang.

3 *to*

We use the preposition *to* to indicate destinations and targets.

See two examples:

- How can I apply for the status of observer *to* the Convention on Tobacco Control?
- The author listed five ways to effectively contribute *to* the cause of environmental protection.

I Fill in the blanks with *for*, *of*, or *to*.

1. I want an opener that can be used _____ opening bottles of beer as well as wine.
2. We are all anxious _____ a quick solution.
3. It reduces volunteerism _____ hours worked instead _____ contribution made.
4. Would you like to go _____ a walk?
5. The students discussed heatedly the value _____ volunteering.
6. Do you get paid extra _____ working on a holiday?
7. This book examines the role, experiences and contribution _____ the volunteers who fought in the battle.
8. A simple act _____ kindness can make a big difference.
9. He is working on a project to provide shelter _____ the homeless.
10. Experts say that climate change poses a threat _____ our oceans.

II Complete the following passage with appropriate prepositions.

Volunteering increases self-confidence. You are doing good _____ others and the community, which provides a natural sense _____ accomplishment. Your role as a volunteer can also give you a sense _____ pride and identity. And the better you feel _____ yourself, the more likely you are to have a positive view _____ your life and future goals. Volunteering is also a great way to gain experience _____ a new field. Your volunteer work might also expose you _____ professional organizations or internships that could benefit your career.

COMMUNICATING

A Viewing: Volunteering for Something

I Get Prepared: Read the passage and fill in the blanks with the words or phrase from the box.

> sustainable   assist   cuts across   links   implementation   promoting   improve

Engineers Without Borders International

Engineers Without Borders International (EWB-I) is an international association of national EWB groups. EWB-I helps the member groups develop their capacity to (1) _____ developing communities in their respective countries. The member groups of EWB-I share the mission to partner with disadvantaged communities to (2) _____ their quality of life through education and (3) _____ of sustainable engineering projects, while (4) _____ global dimensions of experience for engineers, engineering students, and motivated non-engineers. EWB-I creates (5) _____ between these like-minded organizations and (6) _____ national borders. EWB-I is pursuing its vision for a(n) (7) _____ world where engineering enables long-term positive social and global development for the benefit of people and the environment everywhere.

II Get Prepared: You will hear these proper names and words and expressions in the video. Read aloud the proper names in Table 1. Then study the words and expressions in Table 2.

Table 1	Proper Names
Engineers Without Borders	无国界工程师（联合会）
LA Professional Chapter	洛杉矶专业分会
Regional Chapter	地区分会
Boeing	波音公司（世界最大飞机制造商之一）
Chicago	芝加哥
Los Angeles Mayor	洛杉矶市长
Executive Council	执行委员会
The University of Colorado, Boulder	科罗拉多大学博尔德分校

Unit 3 **Volunteering**   75

Table 2　Words and Expressions	
volunteer for sth.	自愿（或义务）做某事
put yourself out there	大胆跨出去，勇于尝试
end up doing	最终做某事，以做某事而告终
entrepreneurial	具有企业家素质的，富于企业家精神的
credibility	信用
rise up	升职，升迁
take up	占用，花费（时间、空间或精力）
keep up	跟上（变化等）；继续做（或提供）
give away	捐赠
better off	境况（尤指经济方面）较好的

III　Watch and Listen for Gist: **Watch the video and circle the correct answers.**

▶ 3.03

1　The speaker mainly wants to _____.

　　a. encourage people to volunteer for something

　　b. stress the importance of EWB

　　c. share with people his work experience at Boeing

2　The speaker's volunteering work was _____.

　　a. criticized

　　b. ignored

　　c. recognized

3　What did Boeing end up doing?

　　a. It trained engineers for volunteering work.

　　b. It strongly supported what EWB did.

　　c. It donated $1.1 billion to EWB.

IV　Watch and Listen for Details: **Watch ▶ 3.03 again and fill in the blanks with the information you hear.**

1　On many occasions, the reason why people do not want to volunteer for anything is that they think it would (1) _____. However, the speaker stresses that if people (2) _____, and find a cause, then the feeling and impact that they get out of working on something without

(3) _____, will have profound effect on the person that they are and the things that they (4) _____ with their lives.

2. The speaker volunteered for EWB for many years because he wanted to do some good work, and _____.

3. The speaker believes that the great thing about volunteering is that it only _____ _____.

4. The speaker was named by Boeing their (1) _____ of the year out of (2) _____ employees.

5. The speaker believes that the things that EWB wants to do are (1) _____ the things that Boeing wants. Thus, Boeing should look at that a little bit more (2) _____.

V Watch and Listen for Implied Meaning: Watch part of the video and circle the correct answers.

▶ 3.04

1. It is easy / not easy for people to find something to volunteer for.
2. People will find it worthwhile / not worthwhile to do volunteer work if they work on it without expecting something in return.

VI Watch and Listen for Language Use: Watch parts of the video again and fill in the blanks with the words you hear.

1. And if you want to look at this in an (1) _____ sort of way, if you want to (2) _____ this problem or working in an industry (3) _____ that problem through volunteering, you could really start to understand the problem more deeply and (4) _____ in talking about that.

▶ 3.05

2. And so basically I went into it and I just—I worked hard on that and I ended up (1) _____ through some of the ranks in the LA Professional Chapter and I (2) _____ in the Regional Chapter. And it was a lot of years where I was trying to (3) _____ a lot of the other engineers at Boeing to (4) _____ me and a lot of people didn't want to do it, because they are afraid that it was going to (5) _____ too much of their time.

▶ 3.06

3. And I got to fly to Chicago and meet with the executives (1) _____ and have lunch with the Los Angeles Mayor and lots of random things like that, but the reason why I wanted to (2) _____ was because, (3) _____, in the whole (4) _____ of using a kind of (5) _____ in a big company, I used that opportunity to talk to Boeing, talk to the management at Boeing and (6) _____ convince them that they need—that the things that Engineers Without Borders wants to do and the things that Boeing wants are kind of (7) _____ and they should kind of look at that a little bit more deeply.

▶ 3.07

4. They started in 2002 and in nine years they started from one (1) _____, one professor, in the University of Colorado, Boulder and in nine years they had 12,000 volunteers as part of their thing and they couldn't quite (2) _____. They also added—funded some board positions on the thing and they (3) _____ $1.1 million in grants to projects. So both EWB and all the communities that EWB supported were (4) _____ as a result of that.

▶ 3.08

B Speaking

Activity 1 Why Do I Want to Do Volunteer Work?

I Complete the speech by filling in the blanks with appropriate expressions. Then listen and check your answers.

🎧 3.09

(1) _____, volunteering for something may bring people a lot of benefits. (2) _____, volunteering is a great way to meet new people, which in itself is an interesting experience. Cute and naughty children, kind and wise old men, busy and serious business men… (3) _____ you want to, you may get to know more about them while doing volunteer work. (4) _____, volunteering is good for your mind and body. It can help you feel happier. Being helpful to others delivers immense pleasure. The more you give, the happier you feel. The social contact aspect of helping and working with others can have a profound effect on your overall psychological wellbeing. Nothing relieves stress better than a meaningful connection to another person. (5) _____, volunteers try their best to help others. This provides a natural sense of accomplishment, pride and identity. That means, the better you feel about yourself, the more likely you are to have a positive view of your life. It would be difficult for a volunteer to view life in a negative way. (6) _____, I strongly (7) _____ that everyone join a volunteer organization, find a position, enjoy your work, and make your community a better place.

II Pair Work: Practice the speech in front of your partner.

III Read the useful expressions aloud.

Useful Expressions for Linking Ideas Together	Useful Expressions for Indicating Cause and Effect
for one thing… for another… first… second… third… to begin with… in addition…, besides…	so, thus, hence, accordingly, consequently because, because of, as for the reason why… is…

Unit 3 **Volunteering** 79

IV Pair Work: Do you want to volunteer? Share what you think with your partner. Use the expressions above to help you.

> I don't want to volunteer for anything as it's too time-consuming.

> But you can harvest a lot by doing good for others and the community.

> For example?

> For example, volunteering gives you the opportunity to meet people from different fields, to practice important skills used in the workplace, such as teamwork, communication, problem solving, project planning, task management and organization.

Activity 2   I Want to Volunteer for…

I Read the information in the chart. Then add one more organization that you know.

Voluntary Organizations			
United Nations Volunteers	The Red Cross	China Student Alliance	International Volunteer
World Wide Opportunities on Organic Farms	Harnas Wildlife	Chinese Young Volunteers Association	China Travel Volunteer—Education Support Group
More: _____			

II **Group Work:** Do you know anything about these voluntary organizations? If you do, share what you know with your partners; if you don't, search the Internet for information and then share it with your partners.

III **Discussion:** What kind of voluntary activities do you want to take part in? You may use the model dialog for help.

3.10

A: Do you want to take part in any volunteer activities in your spare time?

B: Well, I am interested in voluntary work, but I haven't participated in any yet because I am not sure if I have enough time to get myself involved in it.

C: Voluntary work will definitely occupy some of your time, but on the other hand, it may bring you benefits, too. For example, volunteers can have many opportunities to know more about society and the world.

A: Yes, I agree with you. In fact, I'm planning to volunteer for something in the coming winter vacation.

B: What kind of work will it be?

A: I'm not quite sure yet, but I registered on UN Volunteers at the beginning of this semester. And now I'm waiting for further information from them.

C Writing

I Fill in the blanks with phrases from the box to complete the paragraphs. You may need to make necessary changes to some of the phrases.

be impressed with	at large	make a meaningful contribution to
gain experience	acquire new skills	expand one's network of contacts
intrinsic value	reduce volunteerism to	put a dollar figure on
basic concept	give aid to	distort the meaning and spirit of

The (1) _____ of volunteering lies in the fact that it is not measured by economic means, but is more or less intended to (2) _____ other individuals, and to the community (3) _____ as well.

Apart from the contribution, volunteering performs manifold functions to many people. One of the commonest functions is that volunteers wish to (4) _____, and (5) _____ by working at different places and meeting different people so as to pave the way for their future career.

It is their spirit of making contributions to others, not time and labor that volunteers have saved us, that we should attach immense value to, as far as volunteering is concerned. So it is wrong to (6) _____ hours worked.

(7) _____ those in need is an essential part of volunteering. It is a spontaneous act of kindness. That's why the value of volunteerism is enormous for a better community. Any attempt to (8) _____ it is in fact to cheapen the (9) _____. Therefore, we should not (10) _____ volunteering by either paying volunteers money or recruiting volunteers by mandatory means.

II Now write an essay of about 220 words on *The Value of Volunteering*. You may use the phrases from the box above.

TEXT B: How to Find the Right Volunteer Opportunity

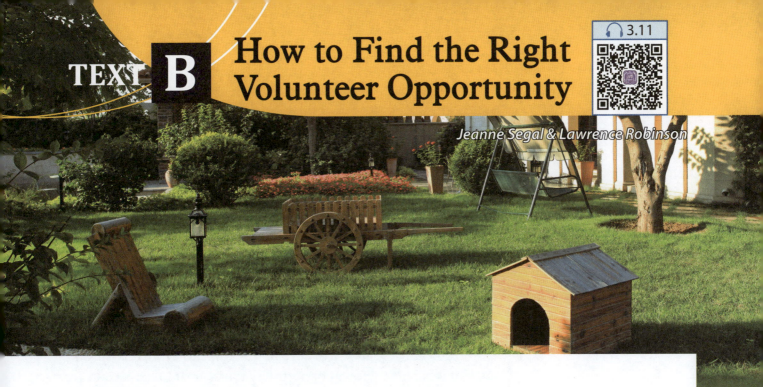

Jeanne Segal & Lawrence Robinson

Volunteering can help you make friends, learn new skills, advance your career, and even feel happier and healthier. Learn how to find the right fit.

Tips for getting started

First, ask yourself if there is something specific you want to do.

For example, do I want

- to improve the neighborhood where I live?
- to meet people who are different than me?
- to try something new?
- to do something with my spare time?
- to see a different way of life and new places?
- to have a go at the type of work I might want as a full-time job?
- to do more with my interests and hobbies?
- to share something I'm good at?

The best way to volunteer is to find a match with your personality and interests. Having answers to these questions will help you narrow down your search.

There are numerous volunteer opportunities available. The key is to find a position that you would enjoy and are capable of doing. It's also important to make sure that your commitment matches the organization's needs. Ask yourself the following:

- Would you like to work with adults, children, animals, or

remotely from home?

- Do you prefer to work alone or as part of a team?
- Are you better behind the scenes or do you prefer to take a more visible role?
- How much time are you willing to commit?
- What skills can you bring to a volunteer job?
- What causes are important to you?

Consider several volunteer possibilities

Don't limit yourself to just one organization or one specific type of job. Sometimes an opportunity looks great on paper, but the reality is quite different. Try to visit different organizations and get a feel for what they are like and if you click with other staff and volunteers.

Where to find volunteer opportunities

- Community theaters, museums, and monuments;
- Libraries or senior centers;
- Service organizations;
- Local animal shelters, rescue organizations, or wildlife centers;
- Youth organizations, sports teams, and after-school programs;
- Historical restorations, national parks, and conservation organizations;
- Online databases.

How much time should you volunteer?

Volunteering doesn't have to take over your life to be beneficial. In fact, research shows that just two to three hours per week, or about 100 hours a year, can confer the most benefits—to both you and your chosen cause. The important thing is to volunteer only the amount of time that feels comfortable to you. Volunteering should feel like a fun and rewarding hobby, not another chore on your to-do list.

Getting the most out of volunteering

You're donating your valuable time, so it's important that you enjoy and benefit from your volunteering. To make sure that

---

remotely adv. 遥远地

shelter n. 避难所

restoration n. 修复处

beneficial adj. 有益的

confer vt. 给予

chore n. 日常琐事

donate vt. 捐献

your volunteer position is a good fit:

Ask questions. You want to make sure that the experience is right for your skills, your goals, and the time you want to spend. Sample questions for your volunteer coordinator might address your time commitment, if there's any training involved, who you will be working with, and what to do if you have questions during your experience.

Make sure you know what's expected. You should be comfortable with the organization and understand the time commitment. Consider starting small so that you don't overcommit yourself at first. Give yourself some flexibility to change your focus if needed.

Don't be afraid to make a change. Don't force yourself into a bad fit or feel compelled to stick with a volunteer role you dislike. Talk to the organization about changing your focus or look for a different organization that's a better fit.

If volunteering overseas, choose carefully. Some volunteer programs abroad can cause more harm than good if they take much-needed paying jobs away from local workers. Look for volunteer opportunities with reputable organizations.

Enjoy yourself. The best volunteer experiences benefit both the volunteer and the organization. If you're not enjoying yourself, ask yourself why. Is it the tasks you're performing? The people you're working with? Or are you uncomfortable simply because the situation is new and unfamiliar? Pinpointing what's bothering you can help you decide how to proceed.

coordinator *n.* 协调者

overcommit *vt.* 过量使用
flexibility *n.* 弹性，灵活性

compelled *adj.* 被强迫的

reputable *adj.* 声誉好的

pinpoint *vt.* 准确指出

Notes

1. **Jeanne Segal & Lawrence Robinson**
   Dr. Jeanne Segal (1939–2017) was a therapist, and an emotional intelligence expert. Over the course of a nearly 50-year career, Dr. Segal, together with her husband Lawrence Robinson, explored the relationship between emotional intelligence and physical and mental health.

2. **after-school programs (Lines 44–45)**
   After-school programs keep kids safe, inspire them to learn and help working families. Volunteers are an integral part of after-school programs. They can serve as mentors, tutors, program assistants, receptionists, and more.

EXERCISES

A Reading for Gist

Answer the following questions according to your understanding of Text B.

1 What are the benefits of volunteering according to the writers?
   _____
   _____

2 What are the writers' suggestions regarding how to find the right volunteer opportunity?
   _____
   _____

B Reading for Details

The following paragraph is a summary of the text. Fill in the blanks with the appropriate words from the text.

Volunteering is (1) _____. However, it doesn't have to take over our life to be so. It should feel like a fun and rewarding hobby, not another (2) _____ on our to-do list. The best way to volunteer is to find a match with our (3) _____ and interests. With numerous volunteer opportunities (4) _____, we should find a position that we would enjoy and are capable of doing. It's equally important to ensure that our (5) _____ matches the organization's needs. We should make sure that the experience is (6) _____ for our skills, goals, and the time we want to spend. When needed, we should give ourselves some (7) _____ to change our focus. And we should (8) _____ ourselves volunteering.

C Reading Beyond

Read the following quotes. Choose one that resonates powerfully with you and then share your understanding with your classmates.

Volunteering is a great way to look outside your own problems. Giving back to makes you happier by both giving you a sense of purpose and helping to put your problems in perspective.
—Karen Salmansohn

I started volunteering at an animal shelter, and little by little, my life started getting better. I think that is the secret. It is just being on a mission that is something bigger than me and it's thankless. You do that because it is thankless, and I am not looking for anybody to say "Thanks" and "You are great!"
—William McNamara

D Prefabs

Write the Chinese meanings of the following prefabs in the text.

have a go at _____

behind the scenes _____

on paper _____

research shows that _____

get the most out of _____

narrow down _____

take a role _____

get a feel for _____

to-do list _____

address one's commitment _____

E Sentence Translation

I Translate the English sentences into Chinese.

1. Volunteering can help you make friends, learn new skills, advance your career, and even feel happier and healthier.

2. The important thing is to volunteer only the amount of time that feels comfortable to you. Volunteering should feel like a fun and rewarding hobby, not another chore on your to-do list.

3. Consider starting small so that you don't overcommit yourself at first. Give yourself some flexibility to change your focus if needed. Don't force yourself into a bad fit or feel compelled to stick with a volunteer role you dislike.

II Translate the Chinese sentences into English, using the expressions in the brackets.

1 不论困难有多大，他都决心去尝试一下这个实验。(*have a go at*)

2 很多名人都领略过贫穷是什么滋味。(*get a feel for*)

3 发达国家必须履行承诺，在减少贫困的同时解决气候变化问题。(*address one's commitment*)

Unit 4 Innovation

Warming Up

Memorize and comment on the following quotations on technology.

1. 中国要强盛、要复兴，就一定要大力发展科学技术，努力成为世界主要科学中心和创新高地。
   —— 习近平

2. The convergence of digital trends, along with the rise of China and globalization, has upended the rules for almost every business in every corner of the globe.
   —Steve Blank

INITIAL READING

A Vocabulary

Read the new words aloud and try to work out their meanings in the text.

New Words

3	**seminal** /'semɪnl/ *adj.*	33	**overstate** /ˌəʊvə'steɪt/ *vt.*
11	**ubiquitous** /ju:'bɪkwɪtəs/ *adj.*	37	**accentuate** /æk'sentʃueɪt/ *vt.*
14	**rotting** /'rɒtɪŋ/ *adj.*	41	**mega** /'megə/ *adj.*
15	**swarm** /swɔ:m/ *n.*	42	**contour** /'kɒntʊə(r)/ *n.*
15	**antique** /æn'ti:k/ *adj.*	43	**disruptive** /dɪs'rʌptɪv/ *adj.*
16	**midland** /'mɪdlənd/ *n.*	45	**crane** /kreɪn/ *n.*
16	**loony** /'lu:ni/ *adj.*	46	**chilling** /'tʃɪlɪŋ/ *adj.*
17	**leech** /li:tʃ/ *n.*	46	**crush** /krʌʃ/ *vt.*
20–21	**thunder-thump** /ˌθʌndə(r) 'θʌmp/ *n.*	48	**utterly** /'ʌtəli/ *adv.*
21	**patriot** /'peɪtriət/ *n.*	51	**patent** /'pætnt/ *n.*
21	**assertion** /ə'sɜ:ʃn/ *n.*	52	**quantum** /'kwɒntəm/ *adj.*
26	**adduce** /ə'dju:s/ *vt.*	56	**drain** /dreɪn/ *vt.*
28	**poised** /pɔɪzd/ *adj.*	58	**retard** /rɪ'tɑ:d/ *vt.*
31	**vassal** /'væsl/ *n.*	58	**crumble** /'krʌmbl/ *vi.*
32	**sanction** /'sæŋkʃn/ *n.*	58	**drunkenly** /'drʌŋkənli/ *adv.*
32	**dominance** /'dɒmɪnəns/ *n.*	59	**defective** /dɪ'fektɪv/ *adj.*

B Skimming

Read Text A and go through the statements within eight minutes. Circle the numbers of the correct statements.

1. With the rapid development of China, America has lost its lead in technology.
2. The rapid development in China surprised the author when he visited China forty years ago.
3. The author stayed in China for about half a month and traveled a lot.
4. Most American people hold the opinion that China always copies inventions from other countries.
5. China moves ahead by leaps and bounds and is currently the only leader in 5G.
6. Now Chinese students are willing to return since Asia is where the action is.
7. It can be inferred from the text that America is yesterday's country and China is no longer backward in technology.
8. The advantages of digging subways outweigh its disadvantages.
9. The U.S. government is clearly aware of the changes of the world.
10. In Para. 9, the author makes a comparison between China and America in a satirical way.

TEXT A — Yesterday's Country: Not to Worry, They Can't Innovate

Fred Reed

For many years the United States has regarded itself as, and been, the world's technological leader. One can easily make a long and impressive list of seminal discoveries and inventions coming from America, from the moon landings to the Internet. It was an astonishing performance. The U.S. maintains a lead, though usually a shrinking one, in many fields. But:

China has risen explosively, from being clearly a "Third World" country forty years ago to become a very serious and rapidly advancing competitor to America. Anyone who has seen today's China (I recently spent two weeks there, traveling muchly) will have been astonished by the ubiquitous construction, the quality of planning, the roads and airports and high-speed rail, the sense of confidence and modernity.

Compare this with America's rotting and dangerous cities, swarms of homeless people, deteriorating education, antique rail, deindustrialized midlands, loony government, and a military sucking blood from the economy like some vast leech, and America will seem yesterday's country. The phrase "national suicide" comes to mind.

A common response to these observations from thunder-thump patriots is the assertion that the Chinese can't invent anything, just copy and steal. What one actually sees is a combination of rapid and successful adoption of foreign technology and, increasingly, cutting edge science and technology. More attention might be in order. A few examples from many that might be adduced:

Though 5G is usually presented as an improvement to smartphones, it is far more, and the Chinese seem poised to jump on it hard. It is interesting that China and South Korea are clear leaders in 5G. The U.S., unable to compete, seeks to prohibit its European vassals from dealing with Huawei by threatening sanctions. Forbes reports Huawei's 5G dominance in the post-American world. Whether Forbes' overstates the facts can perhaps be argued. That China has come from nowhere to be ahead in a crucial technology ought to be a wake-up call. That America has to rely on sanctions instead of better technology accentuates the point.

More than 510,000 overseas students return to China. A couple of decades ago, Chinese students in the U.S. often refused to return to a backward country. It now appears that Asia is where the action is and they want to be part of it.

Chinese bullet trains depend on **mega** bridges. In most countries roads and rails follow the **contour** of the land. China likes pillars. Digging subways is expensive and **disruptive**, cutting highways through cities is destructive of homes and business, so China goes with sky-trains. Building these takes about half the land as roadways. The bridges are built offsite and then erected with a special **crane**.

Chilling World War Ⅲ wargames show U.S. forces **crushed** by Russia and China. The reasons for this are several and belong in another column. The military's **utterly** predictable response is "Send more money" instead of "Maybe we should mind our own business and spend on our economy." The point here is that the world is changing in many ways and Washington seems not to have noticed.

The list could be extended at length, to cover numbers of **patents** awarded, scientific papers published, **quantum** communications, investment in education and technological research and development, supercomputers and chip design and many other things. Beijing is clearly bent on making China great again—as why should it not? Meanwhile America focuses more on transgender bathrooms and whether Bruce Jenner is a girl than on its endless and **draining** wars. China sends its brightest to the world's best technical school while America makes its universities into playpens for the mildly **retarded**. The country **crumbles** but spends **drunkenly** of **defective** fighter planes it doesn't need in the first place.

This won't work a whole lot longer.

Notes

1. **Fred Reed**

   Fred Reed (1945–) is an American freelancer, writer and former technology columnist for *The Washington Times*. He has also written for *The American Conservative* and LewRockwell.com. He currently writes for *Taki's Magazine*, and writes weekly columns for the website "Fred on Everything".

2. **5G (Line 27)**

   5G, also called 5th generation mobile networks, 5th generation wireless systems or 5th-Generation, is the fifth generation wireless technology for digital cellular networks that began wide deployment in 2019. Its goal is to achieve high rate of data transmission, reduction of cost and energy, and connection of large-scale equipment. 5G is conceived for a super connected and super intelligent world. It will become a powerful technology platform inspiring many new applications, new business models and new industries.

3. **Forbes (Line 32)**

   Forbes is a global media company headquartered in New York, focusing on business, investing, technology, entrepreneurship, leadership, and lifestyle. Also, *Forbes*, an American business magazine owned by Forbes, Inc., published biweekly, features original articles on finance, industry, investing, and marketing topics. *Forbes* also reports on related subjects such as technology, communications, science, and law.

4. **Huawei (Line 32)**

   Huawei, a Chinese multinational IT company headquartered in Shenzhen, Guangdong Province, is a leading global provider of information and communications technology infrastructure and smart devices. According to the founder and CEO of Huawei (Ren Zhengfei), the goal of this company is to "build a fully connected, intelligent world".

STUDY READING

A Structure Analysis

Fill in each blank with no more than three words according to your understanding of the structure and content of the text.

	Yesterday's Country: Not to Worry, They Can't Innovate
Introduction (Paras. 1–3)	China has risen from a "Third World" country and become a rapidly advancing (1) _____ to America though the latter regards itself to be and has been the world's technological leader for many years. America seems to be (2) _____ _____.
Transition (Para. 4)	American patriots believe that the Chinese can't (3) _____. Actually, China is successfully and increasingly adopting (4) _____ science and technology.
Body (Paras. 5–8)	The examples are many. • Huawei's 5G (5) _____ the post-American world. • More than half a million of (6) _____ return to China after graduation. • Chinese sky-trains are everywhere. • U.S. forces are (7) _____ by Russia and China.
Conclusion (Paras. 9–10)	China is becoming great again while the U.S. is (8) _____, which the U.S. seems not to have noticed.

B Reading Comprehension

I Sequencing: Identify the order of the following statements according to the text.

_____ A Chinese students would rather stay in America after graduation in the past.

_____ B Americans' landing on the moon was a great achievement.

_____ C More examples can be added to the list of China's advancements.

_____ D Sky-trains are built in China because they take less land.

_____ E The quality of planning and the transport construction in today's China have been astonishing.

_____ F China plays a leading role in 5G technology.

II Blank Filling: Fill in each blank with no more than three words based on the text.

1. Although the U.S. has been on the decline in the world's technology, it still _____.

2. As far as the author is concerned, the current situation in the U.S. makes the phrase "national suicide" _____.

3. As a(n) _____ the fast development of today's China, the American patriots allege that the Chinese can't invent anything.

4. China has not only successfully adopted foreign technologies but also developed _____ science and technology.

5. China is ready to _____ 5G which seems to be an improvement to smartphones.

6. Instead of competing with China, the U.S. _____ prohibit its European partners from dealing with Huawei.

7. The fact that China has taken the lead in the 5G technology should be _____ for the U.S.

8. The Chinese government is _____ making China great again.

III Group Work: According to the text, some American patriots assert that the Chinese can't invent anything, just copy and steal. What's your opinion? Work in groups and discuss it. After the discussion, you are required to recommend a representative to share your ideas in class.

WORD BUILDING

A Prefabs

Exercise 1 Blank Filling: Active Words

I Study the meanings of the active nouns, verbs and adjectives in the table.

Active Words

Title **innovate** /ˈɪnəveɪt/ vi.		To innovate means to introduce changes and new ideas in the way something is done or made.
		one's constant desire to innovate and experiment
5 **maintain** /meɪnˈteɪn/ vt. V n		If you maintain something at a particular rate or level, you keep it at that rate or level.
		to maintain interest rates at a high level
6 **shrink** /ʃrɪŋk/ vi.		If something shrinks, it becomes smaller.
		(the vast forests of West Africa) to have shrunk
13 **confidence** /ˈkɒnfɪdəns/ n.		[U] If you have confidence, you feel sure about your abilities, qualities, or ideas.
15 **deteriorate** /dɪˈtɪəriəreɪt/ vi. V into		If something deteriorates, it becomes worse in some way.
		to deteriorate into full-scale war
17 **military** /ˈmɪlətri/ n.		[C] The military are the armed forces of a country, especially officers of high rank.
19 **suicide** /ˈsuːɪsaɪd/ n.		[U] You say that people commit suicide when they deliberately do something that ruins their career or position in society.
20 **response** /rɪˈspɒns/ n. in N to		[C] Your response to an event or to something is your reply or reaction to it.
		in response to a request from Venezuela
31 **prohibit** /prəˈhɪbɪt/ vt. V n from ving		If a law or someone in authority prohibits something, they forbid it or make it illegal.
		to prohibit pets from entering the hospital
32 **threaten** /ˈθretn/ vt. V n		To threaten is to announce as intended or possible.
		to threaten a strike
35 **crucial** /ˈkruːʃl/ adj.		If you describe something as crucial, you mean it is extremely important.
		the crucial decisions
36 **rely** /rɪˈlaɪ/ vi. V on		If you rely on someone or something, you need them and depend on them in order to live or work properly.
		to rely heavily on the advice of their professional advisers
45 **erect** /ɪˈrekt/ vt. V n		If people erect something such as a building, bridge, or barrier, they build it or create it.
		to erect barricades in roads leading to the parliament building
51 **extend** /ɪkˈstend/ vt. V n		If you extend something, you make it longer or bigger.
		to extend their range

II **Now complete the sentences with the words in the table above. You need to change the form where necessary.**

1. Now that the locals have _____ the town Christmas tree, I find myself looking forward to the holiday season.

2. Face-lifts (去皱整容术) are a classic among older women, possibly because they can boost _____, which, in itself, offers a big career payoff.

3. The U.S. _____ tougher economic sanctions if this country failed to abide by a new international agreement.

4. In the early 19th century, American women were _____ from voting or holding public office and denied access to higher education and the professions.

5. Turkish population figures have doubled since 1970 while Western European states have a(n) _____ population due to low birth rates and an aging population.

6. The two countries agreed to _____ close communication, enhance pragmatic cooperation, and contribute more to world peace and stability in the new year.

7. Increased competition means producers must _____ and improve constantly.

8. As it turned out, no one completed the assignment, so the teacher _____ the deadline by another week.

9. She didn't own a car herself and _____ on public transportation and friends to get around town.

10. "Our youth are increasingly attempting or committing _____ as a result of depression," said Michelle de Sousa, Project Manager of the South African Depression and Anxiety Group.

11. A common measure in _____ to the crisis has been to expand the coverage of unemployment benefits to self-employed workers.

12. Her father, like many able-bodied men in Iraq, was forced to join the _____ in the fight against neighboring Iran and later in the 1991 Gulf War.

13. Her health continued to _____ as aching pain and fever caused sleepless nights.

14. At an emergency EU meeting ministers failed to reach a decision on the most _____ issue—how to distribute 160,000 refugees among the EU countries.

Exercise 2 Prefab Translation

I Discuss the meanings of the following prefabs in the text.

Prefabs

1	regard... as	49	mind one's own business
2	technological leader	51	at length
2–3	make a list of	54	make China great again
24	cutting edge	59	in the first place
38	a couple of decades ago	60	a whole lot

II Translate the following into English, using the prefabs in the table above.

1. 对患有智障的养子视如己出
2. 处于计算机软件技术领先的地位
3. 列出一份大学新生必读书单
4. 日新月异的尖端技术
5. 几十年前的老邻居
6. 叫某人少管闲事
7. 一条有待最终证实的传闻
8. 弘扬振兴中华的民族精神
9. 需要首先解决的主要问题
10. 个头比三年前长高了很多

B Partial Dictation

Listen to the following sentences once only and fill in the blanks with the exact words you hear.

1. The United States still _____ in many fields, though it is already less powerful than before.
2. The rapid development has _____ a potential competitor to America.
3. All the people who have witnessed today's China _____ her latest development in all aspects.
4. Some American patriots have _____ that the Chinese can't invent anything, just copy and steal.
5. China and South Korea _____ 5G race and the U.S. cannot compete with them.
6. The Americans should be aware that China is _____ in a crucial technology like 5G.
7. The construction of Chinese _____ usually traces the contour of the land.
8. Nowadays, China _____ fulfill the prospect of national revival.

C Sentence Translation

Translate the Chinese sentences into English, using the expressions in the brackets.

1. 我在今天报纸头版上看到过的那个新闻标题就是想不起来了。(*come to mind*)

2. 请仔细阅读合同,看看每一条条款是否妥当。(*be in order*)

3. 事实上,优秀的艺术家搞创作远不只是单纯地临摹生活。(*far more*)

4. 全国各地电子商务从无到有,发展迅速。(*come from nowhere*)

5. 她十五岁时不再学习钢琴,开始专注于学业。(*be bent on*)

Translation Tips

Dynamic Equivalents for "Making China Great Again"

The expression "making China great again" in the last but one paragraph of the text could be rendered into the Chinese catchphrase "振兴中华". Noticeably, this phrase is open to a whole lot of other diverse versions in English, for example, "to invigorate China", "to make China powerful and strong", "to make China prosper", "to re-energize China", "to rejuvenate China", "to rejuvenate the Chinese nation", "to revitalize the Chinese nation", "to strengthen China".

Here are some English press clippings to serve as supportive examples for your reference.

- "Rejuvenating China" is the common wishes of the whole nation.

- Each and everyone of us is responsible for the strengthening of China.

- This is important for China facing the new century and is the only road for making China powerful and strong.

- In the meantime, people on both sides of the Taiwan Straits, compatriots of Hong Kong and Macao as well as overseas Chinese and people of Chinese descent all expressed their fervent hope that the two sides of the Straits would join hands to work for the revitalization of China.

- The Chinese people of all ethnic groups, who have taken their destiny in their own hands and enjoy independence, unity, peace and stability, are now able to devote all their energy to the cause of building up their country and realize the lofty ideal of revitalizing the Chinese nation.

Obviously, the phrases and the examples above are cases in point for the various dynamic equivalents for "making China great again", or rather "振兴中华".

As the old saying goes, all roads lead to Rome. The same is true of translating "making China great again". Translation means communicating, so to speak. Or rather, it means translating the meaning, not the words. Judging the validity of a translation cannot stop with a comparison of corresponding lexical meanings, grammatical classes, and rhetorical devices. What is important is the extent to which receptors correctly understand and appreciate the translated text.

GRAMMARING

A subject-verb concord

The subject and the verb phrase agree in number and person, i.e., a singular subject takes a singular verb and a plural subject takes a plural verb. See the following examples:

- The United States *has regarded* itself as the world's technological leader.
- Chinese bullet trains *depend on* mega bridges.

Some nouns ending in *-s* are singular forms, and require a singular verb, e.g., words for games and diseases (*billiards, darts, hepatitis…*), words with the sense of "discipline, field of study" (*mathematics, statistics…*). See the following examples:

- Measles *is* a highly infectious illness caused by a virus.
- The professional ethics *arises* from the requirement that analysis be unbiased.

When a noun phrase contains *more than one* and a singular noun, the verb is normally singular, but when it contains *more than* and a plural noun, the verb is plural. Compare the following examples:

- More than one person *was* involved.
- More than 510,000 overseas students *return* to China.

1 concord with coordinated subjects

We use a plural verb with coordinated subjects connected by *and*. For example:

- It is interesting that China and South Korea *are* clear leaders in 5G.

When the coordinated subject connected by *and* describes a single person or thing, we use a singular verb. For example:

- The creator and champion of the sport *is* injured.
- Corned beef and cabbage *is* an Irish tradition.

Subject noun phrases may be linked by prepositions such as *along with, rather than, as well as*, etc., in which case we use a singular verb when the first noun phrase is singular, and a plural verb when the first is plural. For example:

- The politician, along with the newsmen, *is* expected shortly.
- Women, as well as men, *have* the right to vote.

2 concord with clausal subjects

When the subject is a clause, we usually use a singular verb. For example:

- Building these *takes* about half the land as roadways.
- What one actually sees *is* a combination of rapid and successful adoption of foreign technology.

I Fill in the blanks with the appropriate form of the verbs given in the brackets to complete the sentences.

1. The advent of digitization and electronic media _____ (make) speedy cooperation between us even more necessary.

2. Every adult and every child _____ (be) holding a bag.

3. What is needed _____ (be) effective regulators.

> - Preposed *every* or *each* requires a singular verb.
> - With *what*-clause as the subject, the number of the verb is influenced by the number of the following subject complement.

4. Bacon and eggs _____ (be) my favorite breakfast.

5. It is reported that more than one passenger _____ (be) hurt in a car accident.

6. That America has to rely on sanctions instead of better technology _____ (accentuate) the point.

7. A good knowledge of English, Russian, and French _____ (be) required for this position.

8. Geography, history, and immigration patterns, as well as age and gender distributions of nursing students and the communities they represent, _____ (influence) the particular patterns of enrollment.

II Complete the paragraphs with the appropriate verb forms.

1. In China, elders _____ (be) traditionally treated with enormous respect and dignity while the young _____ (be) cherished and nurtured. In America, the goal of the family _____ (be) to encourage independence, particularly that of the children. Unlike the Chinese, older Americans seldom _____ (live) with their children.

2. Chinese people _____ (have) different meanings to define friends. Just hanging out together time to time _____ (be) not friendship. Friendship _____ (mean) lifelong friends who _____ (feel) deeply obligated to give each other whatever help might seem required. Americans always _____ (call) people they _____ (meet) friends, so the definition of friends _____ (be) general and different. There _____ (be) work friends, playing friends, school friends and drinking friends.

B prepositions: *from, on, with*

1 from

We use the preposition *from* to indicate

- the point in space at which a journey, motion, or action starts;
- the point in time at which a particular process, event, or activity starts;
- the source or provenance of someone or something;
- the starting point of a specified range on a scale;
- separation or removal;
- prevention.

See the following examples:

- One can easily make a long and impressive list of seminal discoveries and inventions coming *from* America, *from* the moon landings to the Internet.
- A common response to these observations *from* thunder-thump patriots…
- China has risen explosively, *from* being clearly a "Third World" country forty years ago to become a very serious and rapidly advancing competitor to America.
- The U.S. seeks to prohibit its European vassals *from* dealing with Huawei by threatening sanctions.

2 on

We use the preposition *on* to

- indicate being physically in contact with and supported by (a surface);
- suggest having… as a topic;
- suggest having… as a target, aim, or focus;
- specify being engaged in;
- indicate the day or part of a day during which an event takes place.

See the following examples:

- The Chinese seem poised to jump *on* it hard.
- That America has to rely *on* sanctions instead of better technology accentuates the point.

3 with

We use the preposition *with* to indicate

- accompanied by;
- having or possessing;

- the instrument used to perform an action;
- the manner or attitude in which a person does something;
- in opposition to;
- in relation to;
- separation or removal from something.

See the following examples:

- The bridges are built offsite and then erected *with* a special crane.
- Compare this *with* America's rotting and dangerous cities.

I Fill in the blanks with prepositions *from*, *on*, or *with*.

1. Tickets for the concert are _____ sale _____ Monday.
2. The finals take place _____ 1:30 p.m. _____ Sunday.
3. Maybe we should mind our own business and spend _____ our economy.
4. Many businesses are developing strategies to deal _____ globalization.
5. While America focuses more _____ transgender bathrooms, Beijing is clearly bent _____ making China great again.
6. A small cloud of smoke rose _____ the glass and the color of the liquid changed _____ red to purple, and _____ purple to a watery green.
7. Prices start _____ £366 per week for a cottage that sleeps four, including a return ferry crossing.
8. As China continues to take a more active role _____ the global stage, it is in an ideal position to partner more closely _____ other developing countries.

II Complete the following paragraphs with appropriate prepositions.

1. _____ a truly remarkable track record, China is undoubtedly a world leader _____ poverty reduction and improving health outcomes and there is a lot the rest _____ the world can learn _____ its experience.

2. China's Belt and Road Initiative (BRI), a massive global program aimed _____ improving inter-connectivity _____ countries, inspired _____ the ancient Silk Road, seeks to boost trade and economic growth _____ Asia and beyond. The BRI will be backed _____ considerable resources. _____ maturity, investments _____ the initiative are expected to hit around $4 trillion, stemming _____ private sources, dedicated funds, and multilateral development banks.

C adjectives ending in *-ing* or *-ed*

There are quite a few adjectives that end in *-ing* or *-ed*. For example:

amusing	amused
boring	bored
confusing	confused
disappointing	disappointed
exciting	excited
frightening	frightened
interesting	interested
relaxing	relaxed
satisfying	satisfied
tiring	tired

The adjective with *-ed* tells us about how a person feels about something. The adjective with *-ing* describes the person or things that have caused that feeling. See the following examples:

- The party is *boring* so we are *bored*.
- The offer was *exciting*. He was *excited* to get it.

Choose the appropriate adjective form to complete the sentences.

1. astonishing, astonished
   a. It was an _____ performance.
   b. The photo shows the president bending over in front of an _____ schoolgirl.

2. relaxing, relaxed
   a. A good warm-up to loosen the body will help you run in a _____ manner.
   b. After I had completed the experiment, I went for a _____ walk.

3. advancing, advanced
   a. Working with peers is critical for _____ learners.
   b. China has become a very serious and rapidly _____ competitor to America.

4. chilling, chilled
   a. The _____ plot of this suspenseful novel moves with amazing quickness.
   b. The U.S. produces, imports and consumes the highest percentage of _____ beef in the world.

5. shrinking, shrunken
   a. The U.S. maintains a lead, though usually a _____ one, in many fields.
   b. His _____ thighs were barely strong enough to support the weight of his body.

COMMUNICATING

A Viewing: China's 5G Network

I **Get Prepared:** Read the passage and fill in the blanks with the words or phrases from the box.

| covering | adding | to raise | improvement |
| rolled out | issuing | in terms of | setting up |

As of the end of March 2022, over 403 million users in China have signed up for 5G plans, which makes China the largest 5G market (1) _____ user size. China's top carriers (2) _____ 5G plans for consumers in November 2019, less than five months after the authority began (3) _____ 5G licenses for commercial use. China's 5G ambition is an integral effort among the government, network carriers, telecoms equipment makers, device makers, and software developers. Policymakers need to show consumers visible (4) _____ on network speed, and as such the carriers have been aggressively (5) _____ 5G base stations across the country—more than 1,559,000 towers, (6) _____ an average of 11,000 new 5G base stations every week. The government has plans (7) _____ that number to 2,000,000 by the end of 2022, (8) _____ all prefectural-level cities nationwide.

II **Get Prepared:** You will hear these words and expressions in the video. Read them aloud.

Words and Expressions	
turbocharge	加速
flirt with	闹着玩似的做；不认真对待
well and truly	肯定；完全，彻底
out in front	处于绝对领先地位
roll out	推出；铺开
connectivity	连通性
latency	延时
instantaneous	即时的

III Watch and Listen for Gist: Watch the video and circle the correct answer.

What is the dialog mainly about?

a. The official launch of the 5G network in China.

b. The superpower status of Chinese economy.

c. The future applications of the 5G technology.

IV Watch and Listen for Details: Watch ▶ 4.03 again and complete the sentences with the information you hear and see.

1 China successfully launched _____ 5G network in the world.

2 Countries including the U.S., _____ and _____ were planning to set up 5G network.

3 As many as _____ million Chinese are estimated to surf the Internet using smartphones.

4 As many as _____ Chinese cities are going to set up 5G network.

5 Distinctive features of the Chinese 5G network include its large _____, low _____ and high _____.

6 One 5G application the female presenter finds interesting is in smart _____ _____.

V Watch and Match Information: Watch part of the video and match the items.

1 How many users in each city are going to have access to 5G network?

Beijing	24,000,000
Shanghai	11,000,000
Guangzhou	21,000,000
Shenzhen	12,500,000

2 What can these applications do with 5G wireless network support?

Smart cars	can detect sickness.
Band aids	can detect each other instantaneously.
Toothbrushes	can detect healing progress.

Unit 4 **Innovation**

VI **Watch and Listen for Language Use:** Watch part of the video and complete the sentences with the exact words you hear.

David Covert is in Beijing for us, (1) _____. We've seen the United States and South Korea (2) _____ this. But this is (3) _____ China (4) _____. Talk us through what was (5) _____ today, David.

But this here in China, it is (6) _____ scale. You know how things are done here in China. It is done (7) _____.

5G is the fifth generation wireless network which could be (8) _____ the current 4G. They are going to be (9) _____ a lot of folks here, millions of people. Let me give you some of the ideas (10) _____ the scale what cities we are talking about. They say some fifty cities are going to be (11) _____.

So that tells you (12) _____ how many millions of people will eventually (13) _____ this.

Latency means the time delay from (14) _____.

B Speaking

Activity 1   What Electronic Media Do You Like?

I Complete the conversation by filling in the blanks with appropriate expressions. Then listen and check your answers.

🎧 4.06

A: (1) _____ electronic media is popular in your hometown?
B: There are some popular kinds: radio, TV and online news.
A: (2) _____?
B: I like online news.
A: (3) _____?
B: It's convenient and easier for me to read online. I work with computers every day.
A: (4) _____ do you read?
B: Every morning before I start working.
A: (5) _____?
B: Instead of watching TV or listening to the radio passively, I'd rather read and think about the news.
A: (6) _____ access all kinds of electronic media?
B: Yes, with a computer, or a smartphone connected to the Internet, you can read electronic news anytime and anywhere.
A: Do your family like electronic media too?
B: Yes. My dad likes radio, and my mom likes TV.

II **Pair Work:** Practice the conversation with a partner.

III Read the useful expressions aloud.

Useful Expressions for Requesting Information			
	Structure	Information Gap	Information
Formal	Could you tell me	when	the next train leaves?
	Do you know	how much	that vase costs?
	Do you happen to know	what	he likes to eat?
	Could you find out	where	the new project is located?
	I'd like to know	why	she does not come.
Casual	Tell me	where	you have been in the last three hours.
	Explain to me	how	this remote control works.
	Inform me	where	we shall meet again.
	Let me know	when	you will return.
	You need to be frank about	what	he is hiding.

IV **Pair Work:** Read the questions below. Add your own question for each situation. Then take turns asking and answering the questions with a partner, using the expressions above to help you.

In a Coffee House	At School
■ Explain to me the difference between latte and cappuccino. ■ How can I access wireless network here? Your question: _____	■ Tell me why you did not return to your dorm last night. ■ Can you explain why you failed to attend my class on Tuesday? Your question: _____
In a Library	**At Home**
■ Could you please show me how this book drop machine works? ■ Would you please demonstrate how to extend the due date on this machine? Your question: _____	■ Tell me why you do not like pizza. ■ Ask yourself how often you drink. Your question: _____

Activity 2 What Is 5G?

I Read the information about 5G in the chart. Add your own findings.

Some Facts About 5G
Speed upgrades Predicted speeds of up to 10 Gbps represent up to a 100x increase compared with 4G.
Low latency 5G latency will be faster than human visual processing, making it possible to control devices remotely in near-real time.
Enhanced capacity 5G will deliver up to 1,000x more capacity than 4G, creating fertile ground for the development of Internet of Things, i.e., IoT.
Increased bandwidth 5G networks are architected differently from traditional 4G networks, allowing greater optimization of network traffic and smooth handling of usage spikes.
Your findings: _____

II Pair Work: Use the information in the chart above and discuss 5G with your partner. You may use the model dialog for help.

A: Could you explain to me what 5G is, please?

B: 5G is the next generation wireless network technology that's expected to change the way people live and work.

A: But can you convince me why we need to choose 5G?

B: Because the benefits of the new technology are expected to fuel transformative new technologies, not just for consumers but also for businesses.

A: Can you elaborate a little bit on the benefits of 5G, please?

B: Much of the hype around 5G has to do with speed. It will have greater bandwidth, meaning it can handle many more connected devices than previous networks. It will enable more connected devices like smart toothbrushes and self-driving cars.

A: Could you please reveal how 5G works?

B: 5G signals run over new radio frequencies, which requires updating radios and other equipment on cell towers. There are low-band, high-band and mid-band networks for different usages, depending on the type of assets a wireless carrier has.

A: Can you tell me how you can actually use 5G now?

B: In order to connect to and get the benefits of a 5G network, consumers have to have 5G-enabled devices.

C Writing

I Fill in the blanks with phrases from the box to complete the paragraphs. You may need to make necessary changes to some of the phrases.

> the sense of confidence
> come to mind
> mind one's own business
> a whole lot
> maintain a lead
> prohibit... from doing
> be bent on
> in the first place
> in order
> compare... with...

An increasing number of people have come to realize the cruel fact that the U.S. wishes to (1) _____ in many fields, by fair means or foul. One of the ways it has been taking is to threaten and impose sanctions against China, who has been rising explosively, thus being seen as a very serious and rapidly advancing competitor to America.

The world has been astonished to see and feel (2) _____ growing and heightened in China, with the ubiquitous construction, bullet trains, 5G smartphones, etc. Many people cannot help (3) _____ what has been happening in China _____ some evidence and phenomena in America to conclude that America is perhaps declining. It is natural that what (4) _____ is perhaps a picture of sharp contrast: growing China and stagnant America.

Rapid development of China is partially due to the fact that China has been attaching special value to advances in science and technology. The world is changing rapidly in many ways and we should understand and adjust ourselves so as to embrace changes. A country, no matter developed or developing, should regard it as the crucial point to (5) _____ doing its own things well (6) _____.

II Now write an essay of about 220 words on *Chinese Dream*. You may use the phrases from the box above.

TEXT B The Functions of WeChat

Larry Romanoff

Since few Americans are familiar with WeChat, let me give you a description. Many of these functions are available in the West through various platforms, but not always to the same extent nor with the same convenience.

With WeChat we can transmit text and voice messages, photos and videos, and other files of any description even of many Mb in size. We can send and receive both text and voice messages in any language because WeChat has an excellent translation function in combination with one of its partners which translates not only text and voice, but will **extract** and translate all text contained in photos, handy for restaurant menus if you can't read Chinese. We can place not only voice calls but video calls to anyone anywhere that transmit over the Internet. It is so convenient that WeChat is the **default** communication choice for a great many people for most purposes. WeChat also has a Moments platform where we can post texts, photos, videos that are visible to those on our contact lists while selecting those who can view and who cannot, reserving some posts for close friends and others more generally public.

In China we have two primary online payment systems, one operated by Alibaba (called Alipay) and the other by WeChat. Its use is nearly universal in China and both are free to the user. During the past several years I cannot recall a single instance where I had cash in my pocket (even small change) when I went anywhere or was shopping for anything. Even to purchase a small bunch of green onions at a street market, the **vendor** has a QR code which my phone scans and the payment into their bank account is automatic.

With WeChat, we can send money to each other. If we

extract *vt.* 提取

default *n.* 默认

vendor *n.* 小商贩

want to share the cost of lunch, you can pay the entire bill and I transfer my share to you through WeChat. If I ever need cash, I could go to any shop or even approach a complete stranger and ask for 1,000 RMB and instantly repay him into his WeChat account. It is frequently used to transfer money internationally this way, sending dollars to a friend in one country and receiving RMB into a WeChat account in China. Instant, secure, and free of all fees. It all happens within a second, with a concurrent text message confirmation from the bank of both sides of the transaction. WeChat is the main reason people can travel anywhere in China with only a mobile phone and passport (and a change of clothing). Through WeChat, people can purchase plane or train tickets, pay taxi fares and hotel bills, restaurant tabs, in the same way.

Another useful WeChat function is real-time GPS location sharing. If a group is traveling to a destination in several cars, WeChat displays an active GPS map showing all locations in real space and time. If I am meeting a friend at a shopping mall or park or other large location, with this GPS function we can see each other's location in real time and I know which way to walk to encounter my friend.

We have WeChat groups which we can create with any number of participants for any convenient purpose. During the COVID-19 "lockdown" in Shanghai we had a temporary WeChat group for the purchase of meat and vegetables that functioned better than any supermarket and with much less trouble. If I want to have a Christmas party I form a group of those I plan to invite, and all our discussions and planning take place within that platform. Most communities (small portions of residential districts) have a WeChat group for notification of community events and sharing important information.

The point with Trump's "sanction" of WeChat is first that it will terminally disrupt international communications between China and the U.S. for students, scientists, diplomats, media reporters, for all those in the U.S. who have frequent communications with China, effects felt more seriously by those in China, which is a plus for Trump. Second, Trump's administration is uncomfortable with the extent to which WeChat is encroaching on the American turf of Twitter, Facebook, WhatsApp, Instagram and more, with already around 100 million downloads in the U.S., and his actions are partially to reclaim that turf by simply banning a competing medium that is threatening to take over and seriously **downgrade** the popularity of similar American platforms.

But most important is the **espionage** and **censorship** role of Trump's **initiative**. As the censorship **noose** tightens around Facebook and Twitter, Americans are naturally moving to WeChat. The real issue is not that WeChat **poses** any danger to the U.S. in any sense but, as with Huawei, the CIA and NSA cannot very well approach WeChat and ask for automatic sharing of all that personal relationship data. Therefore, under the **guise** of China being untrustworthy, the U.S. government simply bans WeChat and thus no one in the U.S. can send or receive any message without the NSA having a copy. A huge plus is that any news not **fitting** the official narrative will then be **strangled** at birth, as Google, Facebook and Twitter are now doing. If Microsoft or another American firm were to buy WeChat, then of course all is well since they are U.S. firms, not Chinese, who automatically share all personal contact data with their government.

downgrade vt. 使降级

espionage n. 间谍活动
censorship n. 审查制度
initiative n. 新措施；倡议
noose n. 套索
pose vt. 造成

guise n. 伪装

fit vt. 符合
strangle vt. 勒死，扼杀

Notes

1. **Larry Romanoff**
   Larry Romanoff was once a visiting professor at Fudan University in Shanghai, presenting case studies in international affairs to senior EMBA classes. He has held senior executive positions in international consulting firms and has written a series of books and articles on China and the West.

2. **Alibaba (Line 21)**
   Alibaba is a leading online wholesale market place for global trade. It is a famous brand of global business-to-business (B2B) e-commerce, providing online merchants with massive business information and convenient online trading market. It is also a community platform for merchants to interact with friends of the chamber of commerce. The mission of Alibaba Group is to make it easy to do business anywhere.

3. **QR code (Line 26)**
   The QR code is a mobile phone readable bar code that can store websites, plain texts, phone numbers, email addresses and any other alphanumeric data. It is a two-dimensional bar code, typically made up of black and white pixel patterns. QR codes are used in a variety of ways including sharing deals and website links.

EXERCISES

A Reading for Gist

Answer the following questions according to your understanding of Text B.

1. What functions does WeChat have according to the text?

   _____
   _____
   _____

2. What results may Trump's sanction of WeChat lead to?

   _____
   _____
   _____

B Reading for Details

Each of the following statements contains information given in the text. Identify and write down the corresponding number of the paragraph from which the information is derived.

1	People can purchase tickets and pay bills through WeChat.	Para. _____
2	Most Americans do not know much about WeChat.	Para. _____
3	WeChat groups are very useful for discussion and notification.	Para. _____
4	Trump's "sanction" of WeChat will cause difficulties that prevent communications between China and the U.S.	Para. _____
5	We can transmit text and voice messages with WeChat.	Para. _____
6	Trump's initiative plays the role of espionage and censorship.	Para. _____
7	WeChat is one of the primary online payment systems in China.	Para. _____
8	There is an active GPS map in WeChat which shows locations in real space and time.	Para. _____

C Reading Beyond

As mentioned in Para. 3, we have two primary online payment systems, one operated by Alibaba (called Alipay) and the other by WeChat. Which one do you prefer and why? Discuss it with your classmates and then present your opinion in class.

D Prefabs

Write the Chinese meanings of the following prefabs in the text.

text and voice message　_____

handy for　_____

over the Internet　_____

online payment system　_____

taxi fare　_____

a plus for　_____

under the guise of　_____

in combination with　_____

video call　_____

contact list　_____

QR code　_____

in real space and time　_____

pose a danger to　_____

E Sentence Translation

I Translate the English sentences into Chinese.

1. WeChat also has a Moments platform where we can post texts, photos, videos that are visible to those on our contact lists while selecting those who can view and who cannot, reserving some posts for close friends and others more generally public.

2. If a group is traveling to a destination in several cars, WeChat displays an active GPS map showing all locations in real space and time.

3. During the COVID-19 "lockdown" in Shanghai we had a temporary WeChat group for the purchase of meat and vegetables that functioned better than any supermarket and with much less trouble.

II Translate the Chinese sentences into English, using the expressions in the brackets.

1. 张先生退休时，公司董事会要我接任首席执行官一职。(*take over*)

2. 他经常假借公司的名义来招摇撞骗。(*under the guise of*)

3. 小狗崽儿一出生就和它们的妈妈分开了。(*at birth*)

Unit 5 Passion

Warming Up

Memorize and comment on the following quotations on taste.

1. 闻多素心人，乐与数晨夕。

—— 陶渊明

2. The happiness of a man in this life does not consist in the absence but in the mastery of his passions.

—Alfred Tennyson

INITIAL READING

A Vocabulary

Read the new words aloud and try to work out their meanings in the text.

New Words

Title **delicacy** /ˈdelɪkəsi/ n.
3 **piercing** /ˈpɪəsɪŋ/ adj.
5 **adversity** /ədˈvɜːsəti/ n.
6 **resentment** /rɪˈzentmənt/ n.
6 **elevate** /ˈelɪveɪt/ vt.
8 **pungent** /ˈpʌndʒənt/ adj.
9 **sedate** /sɪˈdeɪt/ adj.
14 **relish** /ˈrelɪʃ/ n.
19 **apt** /æpt/ adj.
19 **prudence** /ˈpruːdns/ n.
20 **discretion** /dɪˈskreʃn/ n.
21 **irretrievable** /ˌɪrɪˈtriːvəbl/ adj.
24 **deformity** /dɪˈfɔːməti/ n.

26 **sentiment** /ˈsentɪmənt/ n.
28 **exquisite** /ɪkˈskwɪzɪt/ adj.
29 **negligence** /ˈneglɪdʒəns/ n.
29 **absurdity** /əbˈsɜːdəti/ n.
30 **judicious** /dʒuˈdɪʃəs/ adj.
31 **impertinence** /ɪmˈpɜːtɪnəns/ n.
33 **misery** /ˈmɪzəri/ n.
36 **notwithstanding** /ˌnɒtwɪθˈstændɪŋ/ prep.
37 **lament** /ləˈment/ vt.
39 **diversion** /daɪˈvɜːʃn/ n.
40 **partake** /pɑːˈteɪk/ vi.
45 **gratify** /ˈɡrætɪfaɪ/ vt.

B Skimming

Read Text A and go through the statements within eight minutes. Circle the numbers of the correct statements.

1. With a delicacy of passion, people could better perceive happiness and misery.
2. People with much passion are likely to make serious mistakes.
3. Under certain circumstances, a delicacy of passion that one possesses is similar to the delicacy of taste.
4. "People of this character" in Line 5 refer to those who always remain calm in the face of difficulty.
5. People should develop both the delicacy of taste and the delicacy of passion.
6. It is more desirable to have a delicacy of passion than that of taste.
7. We can decide what books to read, what friends to make, but we can't decide what happens in our life.
8. In ancient philosophy, happiness was absolutely dependent on internal factors.
9. One's definition of happiness largely depends on his or her delicacy of sentiment.
10. This essay is mainly about the significance of passion and taste.

TEXT A: Delicacy of Taste and Delicacy of Passion

David Hume

There is a certain delicacy of passion to which some people are subject that makes them extremely sensible to all the accidents of life, and gives them a lively joy upon every prosperous event, as well as a piercing grief when they meet with crosses and adversity. Favours and good offices easily engage their friendship, while the smallest injury provokes their resentment. Any honour or mark of distinction elevates them above measure; but they are as sensibly touched with contempt. People of this character have, no doubt, more lively enjoyments, as well as more pungent sorrows, than men of more cool and sedate tempers. But, I believe, when everything is balanced, there is no one that would not rather choose to be of the latter character, were he entirely master of his own disposition. Good or ill fortune is very little at our disposal; and when a person that has this sensibility of temper meets with any misfortune, his sorrow or resentment takes entire possession of him, and deprives him of all relish in the common occurrences of life, the right enjoyment of which forms the greatest part of our happiness. Great pleasures are much less frequent than great pains, so that a sensible temper must meet with fewer trials in the former way than in the latter. Not to mention, that men of such lively passions are apt to be transported beyond all bounds of prudence and discretion, and take false steps in the conduct of life, which are often irretrievable.

There is a delicacy of taste observable in some men, which very much resembles this delicacy of passion, and produces the same sensibility to beauty and deformity of every kind, as that does to prosperity and adversity, obligations and injuries. When you present a poem or a picture to a man possessed of this talent, the delicacy of his feeling or sentiments makes him be touched very sensibly by every part of it; nor are the masterly strokes perceived with more exquisite relish and satisfaction, than the negligences or absurdities with disgust and uneasiness. A polite and judicious conversation affords him the highest entertainment. Rudeness or impertinence is as great a punishment to him. In short, delicacy of taste has the same effect as delicacy of passion: It enlarges the sphere both of our happiness and misery, and makes us sensible of pains as well as pleasures that escape the rest of mankind.

I believe, however, there is no one who will not agree with me, that notwithstanding this resemblance, a delicacy of taste is as much to be desired and cultivated, as a delicacy of passion is to be lamented, and to be remedied, if possible. The good or ill accidents of life are very little at our disposal; but we are pretty much masters of what books we shall read, what **diversions** we shall **partake** of, and what company we shall keep. The ancient philosophers endeavoured to render happiness entirely independent of everything external. That is impossible to be attained; but every wise man will endeavour to place his happiness on such objects as depend most upon himself; and that is not to be attained so much by any other means as by this delicacy of sentiment. When a man is possessed of that talent, he is more happy by what pleases his taste, than by what **gratifies** his appetites, and receives more enjoyment from a poem, or a piece of reasoning, than the most expensive luxury can afford.

Notes

1. **David Hume**

   David Hume (1711–1776), a Scottish philosopher, historian, economist, and essayist known especially for his philosophical empiricism and skepticism, also made contributions to moral philosophy. Hume's ethical theory continues to influence contemporary philosophers and psychologists interested in topics such as metaethics, the role of sympathy and empathy.

2. **were he entirely master of his own disposition (Line 11)**

   倒装结构，相当于"if he were entirely master of his own disposition"。

3. **which are often irretrievable (Lines 20–21)**

   "which"指上文中的"be transported beyond all bounds of prudence and discretion, and take false steps in the conduct of life"。

4. **as that does to (Line 24)**

   "does"替代上文中的"produces the same sensibility"。

5. **I believe, however, there is no one who will not agree with me, that notwithstanding this resemblance, a delicacy of taste is as much to be desired and cultivated, as a delicacy of passion is to be lamented, and to be remedied, if possible. (Lines 35–38)**

   The pattern "to be done" is repeated three times in this sentence. Repetition is a rhetorical device that purposefully employs a word or phrase for effect, two or more times in a speech or written discourse. The repetition of "to be done" here creates the value of pursuing the delicacy of taste and the delicacy of passion. What's more, the repetition can also make it memorable for the readers.

STUDY READING

A Structure Analysis

Fill in each blank with no more than four words according to your understanding of the text.

People with a delicacy of passion are sensible to prosperity and (1) _____, obligations and injuries. They have more lovely enjoyments as well as (2) _____, and they are apt to (3) _____ in life. Conversely, people with a delicacy of taste are sensible to beauty and (4) _____ of every kind, the former bringing them the highest (5) _____ and the latter great punishment. My view is that a delicacy of taste is to be (6) _____ and cultivated, and a delicacy of passion is to be lamented and remedied. A wise man with (7) _____ obtains more enjoyment from external objects since good or ill fortune is very little (8) _____.

B Reading Comprehension

I Sequencing: Identify the order of the following statements according to the text.

_____ A We have the freedom to choose whatever we want to read.

_____ B Human beings can hardly control their destiny.

_____ C Like delicacy of passion, delicacy of taste also makes us feel both pains and pleasures.

_____ D Some people react to life events in a very sensitive way because of the delicacy of passion.

_____ E According to ancient philosophers, happiness can only be attained from the inner heart.

_____ F There are more great pains than great pleasures in life.

II **Blank Filling:** Fill in each blank with no more than three words based on the text.

1. If one can gain friendship by favors and _____, this kind of friendship may be easily ruined by minor hurt.

2. If one can be affected _____ by personal glory and rank, then any contempt will trouble him.

3. Generally speaking, if a person is master of _____, he usually has a peaceful temper.

4. If a person has a sensitive character, sadness or sorrow will _____ him in adverse situations.

5. People with passions have the tendency to behave recklessly, so they may _____ in daily life.

6. A man with delicacy of his feeling _____ perceive with the pleasure and satisfaction in a poem or a picture.

7. We can't take control of what happens in our life, but we can decide the books we read, the entertainment we take, and the people we _____.

8. The ancient philosophers _____ place happiness on something internal, which is hard to be achieved.

III **Group Work:** According to the text, "a delicacy of taste is as much to be desired and cultivated, as a delicacy of passion is to be lamented, and to be remedied, if possible." How do you understand this idea? Work in groups and have a discussion. Then you are required to recommend a representative to share your ideas in class.

WORD BUILDING

A Prefabs

Exercise 1   Blank Filling: Active Words

I Study the meanings of the active nouns, verbs and adjectives in the table.

Active Words

Title	**passion** /ˈpæʃn/ n.	[U] Passion is a very strong feeling about something or a strong belief in something.
4	**grief** /griːf/ n.	[U] Grief is a feeling of extreme sadness.
5	**provoke** /prəˈvəʊk/ vt. V n	If something provokes a reaction, it causes it. *to have provoked a shocked reaction*
6	**distinction** /dɪˈstɪŋkʃn/ n.	[U] Distinction is the quality of being very good or better than other things of the same type.
7	**contempt** /kənˈtempt/ n.	[U] If you have contempt for someone or something, you have no respect for them or think that they are unimportant.
11	**disposition** /ˌdɪspəˈzɪʃn/ n.	[C] Someone's disposition is the way that he or she tends to behave or feel.
14	**deprive** /dɪˈpraɪv/ vt. V n of	If you deprive people of something that they want or need, you take it away from them, or you prevent them from having it. *to deprive them of the fuel necessary to heat their homes*
23	**resemble** /rɪˈzembl/ vt. V n	If one thing or person resembles another, they are similar to each other. *to resemble his father*
24	**prosperity** /prɒˈsperəti/ n.	[U] Prosperity is a condition in which a person or community is doing well financially.
28	**perceive** /pəˈsiːv/ vt. V n	If you perceive something, you see, notice, or realize it, especially when it is not obvious. *to perceive the need to consider pensions*
29	**disgust** /dɪsˈɡʌst/ n.	[U] Disgust is a feeling of very strong dislike or disapproval.
38	**remedy** /ˈremədi/ vt. V n	If you remedy something that is wrong or harmful, you correct it or improve it. *to remedy the situation*
40	**endeavour** /ɪnˈdevə(r)/ vi. V to v	If you endeavour to do something, you try very hard to do it. *to endeavour to protect labor union rights*
41	**render** /ˈrendə(r)/ vt. V n	You can use render with an adjective that describes a particular state to say that someone or something is changed into that state. *to render it worthless*
41	**external** /ɪkˈstɜːnl/ adj.	External is used to indicate that something is on the outside of a surface or body, or that it exists, happens, or comes from outside. *external allergic reactions*

II **Now complete the sentences with the words in the table above. You need to change the form where necessary.**

1. There was a certain complexity to the music, but it was—without a doubt—filled with _____ and emotion.

2. The manager's _____ for knowledge undermines the work of those who bring expertise to their jobs.

3. He describes the transformation he has undergone since his days of luxurious living, saying that "the _____ things of life seem to me now of no importance at all".

4. Since their inception, statisticians have _____ to improve the quality and accuracy of these statistics.

5. Education is still the number one priority, because the country's future economic _____ depends upon it.

6. The Moscow-trained and London-based violinist Grigory Zhislin is an artist of _____ and imagination.

7. In order to make a creature that even vaguely _____ the comic book version, special effects are obviously necessary.

8. It is important to seek professional help when one feels overwhelmed by _____ or memories.

9. Teacher burnout (过劳) is a disease and must be _____ if productive teaching and learning is a goal.

10. If children are _____ of these experiences, they will not learn to handle the risks that they are certain to meet as they make their way through life.

11. Carol longs for both love and friendship, and uses her sunny _____ to hide an inner loneliness and desire to belong.

12. Some left the cinema half an hour before the end of the film in _____, anger and quite frankly, boredom.

13. Spatial intelligence, the power to _____ form and give visual shape to ideas, is equally important.

14. As can be clearly seen from the poem, love is _____ through different metaphors (隐喻).

15. The exhibit by internationally-renowned artist Jannis Kounellis has succeeded in _____ strong reactions.

Exercise 2 Prefab Translation

I Discuss the meanings of the following prefabs in the text.

Prefabs

1 *a delicacy of*	15 *common occurrence*
2 *sensible to*	33 *sensible of*
4–5 *good offices*	40 *partake of*
7 *with contempt*	41 *independent of*
14 *take possession of*	44 *be possessed of*

II Translate the following into English, using the prefabs in the table above.

1. 对心灵的一种无限微妙的感觉 _____

2. 对气候变化极其敏感的农作物 _____

3. 请求第三国斡旋，协助解决争端 _____

4. 嗟来之食 _____

5. 企图将公共财物据为己有 _____

6. 胜败乃兵家常事。 _____

7. 认识到自己的缺点和错误 _____

8. 和同事共进工作午餐 _____

9. 不以人的意志为转移的客观规律 _____

10. 具备市场竞争意识 _____

B Partial Dictation

Listen to the following sentences once only and fill in the blanks with the exact words you hear.

1 Delicacy of passion can _____ on every good fortune.

2 If you _____ and offer the help for some people's achievement, you can easily own their friendship.

3 Sensitive people experience more satisfaction and more griefs than people with _____.

4 When people with sensitive temper _____ any misfortune, their sorrows control them completely.

5 Passionate people _____ break the bounds of prudence and discretion and cause unfavorable outcomes.

6 Delicacy of taste resembles delicacy of passion and they _____ of our joys and pains.

7 People hold the opinion that the delicacy of taste can be _____.

8 The ancient sage _____ interpret happiness internally regardless of the external influence.

C Sentence Translation

Translate the Chinese sentences into English, using the expressions in the brackets.

1 从某种意义上说，人是受各种环境支配的。(be subject to)

2 图书馆里有大量的知识任你使用。(at one's disposal)

3 他有一所大房子和一辆豪车，且不说在郊区还有一栋别墅了。(not to mention)

4 食物在夏天容易变质，不宜久放。(be apt to)

5 可能的话，我更喜欢喝一杯珍珠奶茶。(if possible)

Translation Tips

"Not to Mention" and Its Near Expressions

The last sentence in Para. 1 of the text goes: "Not to mention, that men of such lively passions are apt to be transported…". The underlined expression "not to mention" is used when you want to introduce an additional fact or point which reinforces the point being made, or to emphasize something that you are adding to a list. Among its equivalents in Chinese are "更不用说", "且不说", and the like.

Practically, in addition to "not to mention", the Chinese expression "更不用说" can be translated into many other close or near expressions in English, such as "needless to say", "let alone", "much less", "say nothing of", "not to speak of". Here are some supportive examples for illustration:

- Needless to say, a good dictionary is a must for all language students.
- I don't know algebra or geometry, let alone calculus.
- He can't discipline himself, much less set a good example for his children to follow.
- Life was suddenly full of possibilities, say nothing of a few unexpected surprises.
- The rent had to be paid, not to speak of school fees.

Just a kind reminder again: All of the underlined words and phrases in the examples above are more or less the same in meaning as "not to mention". In other words, you may feel free to put into English the Chinese phrase "更不用说" by using the expressions if and when necessary under certain circumstances.

GRAMMARING

A existential *there*

The "*there + be + NP*" construction is used to assert the existence of something. The word "there" has no meaning in itself—its function is to put the real subject (NP) in a more prominent position, i.e., the latter half of the sentence. For example:

    There   is   a delicacy of taste observable in some men.
  (formal subject)   (notional subject)

Here are more examples:

- *There is* no one that would not rather choose to be of the latter character.
- For all the compasses in the world, *there's* only one direction, and time is its only measure.

> - The noun following "there be" often has an indefinite specific reference.
> - A singular form of "be" is used when the noun is singular, and a plural form of "be" is used when the noun is plural.
> - If the noun phrase consists of two or more nouns, we use a singular verb when the first noun is singular or uncountable, and we use a plural verb when the first noun is plural.

In formal or literal writing, the verbs below can be used instead of "be" to say that something exists or happens:

                appear
                arise
                come
                emerge
  there +   *exist*   *+ NP*
                remain
                follow
                stand
                occur
                …

Here are two examples:

- *There followed* a long silence.
- *There comes* a time in a person's life when childhood fantasies end and reality begins.

> In the existential sentence, we do not use verbs indicating disappearance or nonexistence.

I Rewrite the following sentences using *there*.

1 You can do nothing.

2 We find a good spirit in this company.

3 All will agree with me.

4 The question of precisely what is meant by lack of competitiveness remains.

5 With the growth of tourism, a new urge to travel abroad arises.

6 Some people are subject to a certain delicacy of passion.

7 Over the years innumerable accidents and incidents have been caused by the airbrakes opening in flight.

8 Do you have any sufficient reason to interfere with the choice which he actually made?

II Correct errors, if any, in the following sentences.

1 There's the limit to what a man can do.

2 There disappears ship after ship.

3 It's no point crying over spilled milk.

4 There is 25,000 species in the orchid family and around 50 native orchids in Britain.

III Complete the following sentences.

1 There is a _____.
2 There is no _____.
3 There is always _____.
4 Where there is a will, there _____.
5 While there is life, there _____.
6 There are _____.

B *as… as*: comparing equal amounts

We use *as… as* structure to say that two items we are comparing have equivalent aspects of quality or manner. For example:

- She looked formidable then, almost *as* formidable *as* her mother.

We use *not as… as* or *not so… as* to make comparisons between things that aren't equal. For example:

- The second race was *not* quite *as* easy *as* the first one.
- There is*n't* anyone *so* blind *as* those who will not see.

1 *as + adj. + NP + as*

A singular noun is used in the "*as* + adj. + NP + *as*" construction, and the adjective precedes the indefinite article *a/an*. For example:

- It was *as lively a discussion as* we thought it would be.
- Rudeness or impertinence is *as great a punishment* to him.

2 *as much… as*

We use *as much… as* or *as many… as* to talk about quantity. For example:

- There were only one-tenth *as many* drill breakages *as* before.
  (plural noun)
- They have produced twice *as much* sugar *as* in the previous season.
  (uncountable noun)

As much can be used adverbially to refer to an action or state. For example:

- He was *as much* interested in music *as* ever.
- You ought to rest *as much as* possible.
- A delicacy of taste is *as much* to be desired and cultivated, *as* a delicacy of passion is to be lamented, and to be remedied.

I Fill in the blanks with *as many* or *as much*.

1   Emily has _____ books as her brother.

2   You know _____ about physics as I do.

3   We have _____ students in our class as we had last term.

4   Grandfather claimed to have _____ medals as the general.

5   I always have a great time when Lily's around—she's _____ fun as a barrel of monkeys!

6   He likes football _____ as he likes basketball.

7   They try to interview _____ candidates as possible.

8   There is ten times _____ traffic in Boston as in New Bedford.

9   Now that he has retired, Robert has at least four times _____ free time as he had last year.

10 Don't thank me; I would do _____ for anyone.

II Rewrite the following sentences, using the "*as* + adj. + NP + *as*" construction.

1   Metal is a better conductor than water.
    _____

2   She is a good cook. So am I.
    _____

3   The problem is not as big as you might think.
    _____

4   This result was better than they expected.
    _____

COMMUNICATING

A Viewing: Audrey Hepburn

I Get Prepared: The video shows an interview with Audrey Hepburn. Read the passage and fill in the blanks with the words from the box.

| to | from | for | as | against | on | during | after | by | under |

Audrey Hepburn was born (1) _____ an English father and a Dutch mother in Belgium in 1929. Their divorce in 1935 was very traumatic (2) _____ young Audrey. In 1939, her mother moved her to the Netherlands, where she thought they would be safe (3) _____ Nazi invasion. However, in 1940, the Netherlands fell (4) _____ Nazi occupation, during which shootings (5) _____ reprisals were common. (6) _____ a young girl, Audrey suffered from constant starvation and witnessed her uncle and cousin shot dead in the street (7) _____ the Germans. The experiences of war left a profound mark (8) _____ Audrey, leading to her later commitments to the United Nations International Children's Emergency Fund, abbreviated as UNICEF. (9) _____ the war, Audrey went to London where she continued to practice ballet, but her undesirable physical conditions due to the malnutrition (10) _____ the war meant that she was unable to become a really great ballerina, and so she decided to seek an acting career in which she achieved much fame.

II Get Prepared: You will hear these proper names and words and expressions in the video. Read aloud the proper names in Table 1. Then study the words and expressions in Table 2.

Table 1 Proper Names	
UNICEF (United Nations International Children's Emergency Fund)	联合国儿童基金会
Ecuador	厄瓜多尔
Andes	（南美洲）安第斯山脉
UNRRA (United Nations Relief and Rehabilitation Administration)	联合国善后救济总署

Table 2	Words and Expressions
entail	牵涉；势必带来
field trip	实地察看
snowball	滚雪球般增长
advocacy	宣传；游说
amass	收集
immunization	免疫
malnutrition	营养不良
impair	损害
lie in ruins	成了一片废墟，满目疮痍
reprisal	报复

III Watch and Listen for Gist: Watch the video and arrange the presenter's questions in the order they are asked. Do you think Audrey Hepburn is a lady of both taste and passion?

A Was UNICEF that type of organization?
B How about the effect that was on your family, for example, your immediate family?
C As a young girl, did you get involved in any way in the resistance movement?
D What exactly does the job entail?
E Did you know how massive the job was going to be when you took it on?
F Does all of that come easy to you?

sequence: _____

IV Watch and Listen for Details: Watch part of the video and circle the correct answers.

1 The job of a special ambassador for UNICEF was mostly like _____.
   a. a messenger   b. a tourist   c. an observer

2 Audrey Hepburn flew around the world to make people aware of _____.
   a. the needs of UNICEF
   b. disadvantaged children
   c. African development

3. Audrey Hepburn was not entirely prepared for the job at the beginning because _____.
   a. it was a snowball of adversity
   b. there were increasing needs of children
   c. it involved extensive publicity tasks

4. Audrey Hepburn thought _____.
   a. people in power and a higher place launched lovely projects
   b. the inauguration address of Ecuadorian president was very convincing
   c. the president of Ecuador was firmly committed to children

5. The pro-Andes project had _____ countries united for a common good.
   a. nine   b. five   c. four

6. The problems facing children which Hepburn mentioned in this clip are _____.
   a. immunization, poverty and education
   b. funding, know-hows and organization
   c. education, immunization and organization

V Watch and Match Information: Watch part of the video and fill the phrases (a–h) in their corresponding sentences.

▶ 5.05

a. jet lag and travel
b. what should be done to children
c. what has been done to children
d. investments in armament and economy
e. loving children
f. assistance to the fragile and the vulnerable
g. malnutrition and health impairments
h. wartime occupations

Audrey Hepburn thought of	with an uneasy feeling.
	with an easy feeling.
Audrey Hepburn observed	with a light heart.
	with a heavy heart.
Audrey Hepburn believed	is an urgent matter.
	is of secondary importance.
Audrey Hepburn experienced	similar to those unprivileged children.
	different from those disadvantaged children.

VI Watch and Listen for Language Use: Watch part of the video and fill in the blanks with the word and phrases from the box.

 5.06

> taken as hostages once more or less
> something like shot as a reprisal bringing around
> you know considering that lay in ruins
> little fantasies

Hepburn: UNRRA was the forerunner of UNICEF. It was the United Nation's organization that helped children in Europe then. (1) _____ those children were taken care of, they went on to take care of the children in the developing countries. But if you think that war-ravaged Europe, you know, when really Europe (2) _____, and there was (3) _____ 20 million people homeless, the amount of children.

Hepburn: Well, my two brothers, one was hidden (4) _____. The other was taken to Germany. He was a student. I also lost some members of my family, because they were (5) _____, and (6) _____, for something the underground had done and everything, but that happened a lot.

Hepburn: Some stories have been exaggerated about my contribution, (7) _____ messages occasionally, because there was nobody else to do it, (8) _____.

Presenter: But as a child, and (9) _____ you had very little food, and you said you were mal-nourished, what sort of dreams of food did you have, or (10) _____?

B Speaking

Activity 1 — What Are You Talking About?

 5.07

I Listen to the conversation and fill in the blanks with what you hear. How does Max avoid a confrontation with Jack?

Max: Jack, what's wrong?

Jack: You!

Max: What are you talking about? What did I do?

Jack: You told Martha that I was on a date? (1) _____?

Max: No… (2) _____. I didn't mean that. She asked me where you were and I jokingly said that you were on a date with Sara. I thought Martha knew that you and Sara were just friends.

Jack: She started feeling suspicious after you said that.

Max: I'm sorry, man. I didn't know. (3) _____.

Jack: Martha gets jealous easily and it took a while to convince her that Sara was just a friend. Now, I have to explain to Sara that I can't hang around with her because of you.

Max: Look. (4) _____, and next time I see Martha, I'll really tell her that you and Sara are really just friends.

II Pair Work: Practice the conversation with a partner.

III Read the useful expressions aloud.

Useful Expressions for Avoiding a Confrontation		
Clarify a Situation	**Establish Connection**	**Find the Issue**
■ That's not what I meant. ■ I didn't mean that. ■ I didn't mean to… ■ I really didn't mean to…	■ I'm with you on that… ■ I understand your problem… ■ I realize why you're upset… ■ It may not be your fault… ■ I believe your story…	■ Tell me what irritates you. ■ Help me understand why you… ■ Please, explain what you mean. ■ Don't you think that…? ■ Do you find that…?
Make an Apology	**Ask for / Offer Suggestions**	**Reach an Agreement**
■ I'm sorry. I didn't know. ■ I'm sorry. It's my fault. ■ I apologize for that. ■ I apologize for doing… ■ I apologize for being… ■ I apologize.	■ How can I fix this? ■ What can we/I do? ■ Is there anything I can do to…? ■ Do you think you can…? ■ If I were you… ■ Let's look at this from a different perspective.	■ It's been worse than this. We'll get through it! ■ Let's work on this problem together! ■ Even if you did not mean to…, you should not have…, so…

IV **Pair Work: Student A is facing Student B. Choose one of the situations below (or one of your own). Role play the situation. Then switch roles.**

Situation 1	**A** intends to tell **B** that **A** knows that **B** cheated **A**.
Situation 2	**B** broke **A**'s laptop but refused to confess what he or she did.
Situation 3	**A** found that **B** committed plagiarism in his or her homework.
Situation 4	**A**'s submission of a team assignment was delayed by **B**'s late work.

Activity 2 Unwelcome Questions

I There are many ways to avoid answering a question you do not want to answer. Rank the politeness of the expressions below by marking either polite or impolite.

polite/impolite	No comment. Wait and see.
polite/impolite	I'm sorry, but that's confidential. I'm sorry, but that's personal.
polite/impolite	I'd rather not talk about it. I'm not at liberty to say that.
polite/impolite	Let me get back to you later. Why do you want to know that?
polite/impolite	Mind your own business. It's none of your business.

II **Pair Work:** Student A asks two or three questions and Student B avoids answering them. Then switch roles. You may use the model dialogs for help.

5.08

A: Could you explain what you did with your new book, please?

B: I'm sorry, but that's personal.

A: But can you damage a new book like that?

B: It's my book. I can do whatever I like with it.

A: But isn't it a book of good value?

B: It's none of your business.

B: I wonder why you dated that boy.

A: Why do you want to know that?

B: Isn't he dating Lee's girlfriend these days?

A: I'd rather not talk about this.

B: But don't you think that you'd get hurt if that's true?

A: I'll just wait and see.

C Writing

I Fill in the blanks with phrases from the box to complete the paragraphs. You may need to make necessary changes to some of the phrases.

be subject to	good offices	no doubt
good fortune	at one's disposal	take possession of
deprive sb. of sth.	not to mention	take false steps
conduct of life	keep company of	be possessed of

It is believed that to sense and sensibility all of us (1) _____ to varying degrees. Generals and statesmen are normally prone to reason and often show intellectual sense while poets and artists are prone to feeling and (2) _____ delicate sensibility or taste and strong emotion or passion. Now allow us to dwell on the issue of passion a little bit, with an artist as an example.

When an artist has sufficient passion, he can create magnificent works on the subject he is familiar with. Then he feels on top of the world and enjoys wind-like freedom as if everything were (3) _____. However, when he lacks sufficient passion, he feels that everything is so dry and drab and feels himself (4) _____ the very gift nature grants him. He can do nothing, (5) _____ great artistic creativities. (6) _____, passion is vital to a great artist.

However, the artist is in most cases sensibly touched. As he tends to have more lively joys so he is inclined to suffer more pungent sorrows. The problem is that life is filled with ups and downs. His moods show all the ebb and flow of his inner life. We often see that (7) _____ makes a great artist while ill fortune mars him. So if one wishes to score remarkable achievements as an artist, he should learn to master his passion, which enables him not to let his sorrow or resentment (8) _____ him when he finds himself in trying circumstances. He should be careful enough not to (9) _____ in the (10) _____, for the false step might lead to dire and disastrous consequences.

II Now write an essay of about 220 words on *Taste and Passion*. You may use the phrases from the box above.

TEXT B A New Sensation: Recording and Reproducing Taste

Steve Nadis

In 1877, Thomas Edison invented the **phonograph**, becoming the first person ever to record and reproduce his own voice. In 1895, the Edison Company created one of the earliest sound "movies"—a 17-second clip that showed one man playing a violin while two others danced nearby. For 125 years, in other words, it has been possible to record audio and visual scenes and play them back with reasonably high **fidelity**. But in the entire history of humanity, there has been no way of recording and reproducing the taste of a food or **beverage**—that is until last year with the **advent** of Homei Miyashita's "Taste Display". The invention by Miyashita, a scientist in Tokyo, is a 21st-century **analogue** of a phonograph—one that plays back tastes rather than sounds.

Miyashita has a longstanding interest in food and taste. His curiosity about ingredients was piqued as a child when his mother wrote a recipe book. He has carried out his own research which explores the **interface** between technology and the human senses. In 2012, he and a former PhD student developed an "electric fork" that was originally intended to enhance the flavor of hospital food—the idea being to make food taste saltier, for instance, without actually adding salt, thereby avoiding possibly **adverse** health consequences.

That was an early step for Miyashita, who had bigger, more ambitious plans. Whereas the electric fork could make food taste saltier or sourer, the Taste Display could reproduce any flavor one might care to **conjure** up. Here's how it works, starting with a bit of **anatomy**: The human tongue has separate **receptors** for detecting the five basic tastes—sweet, sour, bitter, salty, and **umami**. Miyashita's device has five different gels, each containing an electrolyte solution that causes the tongue, upon contacting the surface, to sense one of those flavors at an intensity that is readily adjustable. Each gel is connected to a separate (exceedingly weak) electric current, and the taste associated with that gel diminishes when the current is turned up. A sixth, tasteless gel is also included as a buffer that keeps the overall current level—and the associated stimulation of the tongue—constant at all times.

By adjusting the current strengths for all six gels, which can be done automatically, the taste of a chocolate milkshake or a sirloin steak or any other desired treat can be experienced through the use of this device without any caloric intake.

The Taste Display initially took the form of a rod that resembles a hand-held microphone with a surface that's designed to be licked rather than talked into. But Miyashita already has an early version of a mask, which affords a user continuous contact with the flavor-imparting surface, as part of a virtual reality system. He also has developed a "lickable screen" that can be incorporated onto a cell phone, allowing a person to watch a cooking show, for example, while tasting various samples.

"Or someone looking at a recipe on a website could find out what that dish tastes like," he says. "We now have smartphones with cameras, displays, microphones, and speakers. But we'll soon be able to go further and upload and download our taste experiences."

That's a brief introduction to the taste reproduction part of the story, but what about the recording end of things? Miyashita is currently using commercially available "taste sensors" that provide a quantitative measure of the five flavor components of any food that is sampled. He developed equations that convert that taste data into a corresponding current strength for each of the five flavors.

Present-day taste sensors are bulky machines that are rather slow at turning out results. Miyashita is exploring faster, more portable ways of taste recording—perhaps through the use of a thermometer-like device that can be dipped into food, giving quick readouts of the distinct flavor components. A portable "salt-meter" like this already exists, and it could be adapted to measure other flavors too. Within 10 years, he predicts, we should be able to instantly record and reproduce taste information.

electrolyte n. 电解质

diminish vi. 变小；减弱
buffer n. 缓冲区

milkshake n. 奶昔
sirloin steak 西冷牛排
caloric intake 热量摄入

impart vt. 传送

incorporate vt. 将……安装在内

quantitative adj. 定量的

bulky adj. 庞大的

thermometer n. 体温计

Unit 5 Passion 143

myriad *adj.* 无数的
gustatory *adj.* 味觉的

texture *n.* 口感；质地

Eating, however, is about more than just sensing the five basic flavors in their myriad combinations. Smell is also an important part of the gustatory experience, and Miyashita is already experimenting with "smell displays". He's also looking into the sensation of touch, examining how a particular food feels in your mouth. To this end, he's working on 3D printing, using not just smooth plastic but a range of materials that have varying degrees of roughness. "By combining that with our taste research," he says, "we hope to reproduce the texture you feel while eating."

"But there's only so much you can do," he admits. "You could watch a travel video, but that probably won't eliminate your desire to visit a foreign land. Nor would listening to a record necessarily satisfy your urge to hear live music." And so, too, it is with taste. Technology can, of course, do marvelous things—his lab being a prime example. But there's also something to be said for a good home-cooked meal, Miyashita says, perhaps drawn from the pages of his mother's recipe book.

> **Note**
>
> **Steve Nadis**
> Steve Nadis is a freelance writer living in Cambridge, Massachusetts, U.S.A. As a columnist of the journal *Astronomy*, he has been a researcher of MIT and the Union of Concerned Scientists, and a consultant of institutions such as the World Resources Institute (WRI) and Public Broadcasting Service (PBS).

EXERCISES

A Reading for Gist

Answer the following questions according to your understanding of Text B.

1. Why did the author say that the invention by Miyashita is a 21st-century analogue of a phonograph?

   _____
   _____

2. How does Miyashita reproduce the food sensation of smell and touch?

   _____
   _____

B Reading for Details

Each of the following statements contains information given in the text. Identify and write down the corresponding number of the paragraph from which the information is derived.

1. Human beings may be able to record and reproduce taste information in a decade.   Para. _____
2. The human tongue could discover five basic tastes.   Para. _____
3. The taste of a food or beverage couldn't be recorded and reproduced in the past.   Para. _____
4. A special screen can help people taste the food samples while watching a cooking show.   Para. _____
5. The interface between technology and the human senses is studied by Miyashita.   Para. _____

C Reading Beyond

Recording and reproducing food senses is a very interesting topic. Discuss with your group members and share your opinions about the significance of the invention mentioned in the text with the whole class.

D Prefabs

Write the Chinese meanings of the following prefabs in the text.

play sth. back　　　　　　　　　　　_____

electric current　　　　　　　　　　_____

virtual reality　　　　　　　　　　　_____

experiment with　　　　　　　　　　_____

live music　　　　　　　　　　　　　_____

in the entire history of humanity　　_____

take the form of　　　　　　　　　　_____

convert sth. into　　　　　　　　　　_____

to this end　　　　　　　　　　　　　_____

a prime example　　　　　　　　　　_____

E Sentence Translation

I Translate the English sentences into Chinese.

1. Miyashita is currently using commercially available "taste sensors" that provide a quantitative measure of the five flavor components of any food that is sampled.

2. Present-day taste sensors are bulky machines that are rather slow at turning out results.

3. You could watch a travel video, but that probably won't eliminate your desire to visit a foreign land. Nor would listening to a record necessarily satisfy your urge to hear live music.

II Translate the Chinese sentences into English, using the expressions in the brackets.

1. 生命是一部永远也无法回放的绝版影片。(*play back*)

2. 这段黄金岁月因为第二次世界大战的到来而结束了。(*with the advent of*)

3. 劳驾，您能把电视机的声音调大一点吗？(*turn up*)

Unit 6 Language Learning

Warming Up

Memorize and comment on the following quotations on language learning.

1. 学外语，要眼尖、耳明、嘴勤、手快。只要多读、多记、多讲、多写，自有水到渠成之日。

   ——许国璋

2. Language study is a route to maturity. Indeed, in language study as in life, if a person is the same today as he was yesterday, it would be an act of mercy to pronounce him dead and to place him in a coffin, rather than in a classroom.
   — John A. Rassias

INITIAL READING

A Vocabulary

Read the new words aloud and try to work out their meanings in the text.

New Words

7	**haphazard** /hæp'hæzəd/ *adj.*	40	**accompany** /ə'kʌmpəni/ *vt.*
9	**playmate** /'pleɪmeɪt/ *n.*	42	**scorching** /'skɔːtʃɪŋ/ *adj.*
13	**mastery** /'mɑːstəri/ *n.*	51	**overlook** /ˌəʊvə'lʊk/ *vt.*
32	**genuine** /'dʒenjuɪn/ *adj.*	54	**sprinkle** /'sprɪŋkl/ *vt.*
35	**ever-bubbling** /'evə(r) 'bʌblɪŋ/ *adj.*	55	**plunge** /plʌndʒ/ *vt.*
36	**assimilation** /əˌsɪmə'leɪʃn/ *n.*	57	**elaborate** /ɪ'læbərət/ *adj.*

B Skimming

Read Text A and go through the statements within eight minutes. Circle the numbers of the correct statements.

1. By comparison, we can better understand why children acquire their mother tongue well.
2. The children could learn their mother tongue well because they are instructed systematically.
3. Talented children rarely make mistakes in language learning.
4. The flexibility of children's organs of speech perfectly explains why they perform better in language learning.
5. Only one decisive factor influences children's language learning ability.
6. The prime time of first language acquisition is in the first years of children's life.
7. What a child hears is usually what immediately interests him.
8. A child's "teachers" always repeat their words and use gestures in order to make their teaching interesting.
9. "Unfortunately" (in Para. 8) is a function word, which indicates that the author is going to point out something disappointing.
10. Mastery of detailed rules of grammar enables one to acquire a foreign language efficiently.

TEXT A: Why Is the Native Language Learnt So Well?

Otto Jespersen

How does it happen that children learn their mother tongue so well? Let us compare them with adults learning a foreign language, for the comparison is both interesting and instructive.

Here we have a little child, without knowledge or experience; there a grown-up person with fully developed mental powers. Here a haphazard method of teaching; there the whole task laid out in a system. Here no professional teachers, but parents, brothers and sisters, nurses and playmates; there teachers specially trained to teach languages. Here only oral instruction; there not only that, but textbooks, dictionaries and visual aids.

And yet this is the result: here a complete mastery of the language however stupid the children; there, in most cases, even with people otherwise highly gifted, a faulty and inexact command. What accounts for this difference?

Some people believe that a child's organs of speech are more flexible than an adult's. This explanation, however, does not really hold water. Children do not learn sounds correctly at once, but make countless mistakes. Their flexibility of the tongue and lips is acquired later, and with no small difficulty.

Others argue that a child's ear is especially sensitive. But then the ear also needs training, since at first it can hardly detect differences in sounds which grown-up people hear most clearly.

The real answer in my opinion lies partly in the child himself, partly in the behavior of the people around him. In the first place, the time of learning the mother tongue is the most favorable of all, namely, the first years of life. A child hears it spoken from morning till night and, what is more important, always in its genuine form, with the right pronunciation, right intonation, right use of words and right structure. He drinks in all the words and expressions which come to him in a fresh, ever-bubbling spring. There is no resistance: There is perfect assimilation.

Then the child has, as it were, private lessons all the year round, while an adult language-student has each week a limited number of hours which he generally shares with others. The child has another advantage: He hears the language in all possible situations, always **accompanied** by the right kind of gestures and facial expressions. Here there is nothing unnatural, such as is often found in language lessons in schools, when one talks about ice and snow in June or **scorching** heat in January. And what a child hears is generally what immediately interests him. Again and again, when his attempts at speech are successful, his desires are understood and fulfilled.

Finally, though a child's "teachers" may not have been trained in language teaching, their relations with him are always close and personal. They take great pains to make their lessons easy and interesting, always repeating the same phrases and at the same time doing the thing they are talking about. They are greatly pleased at every little advance the child makes. Every awkward attempt meets with sympathy and encouragement and the most difficult step on the path of language becomes the merriest game. Unfortunately, this is a point often **overlooked** by teachers of language who demand faultless accuracy from the beginning. By keeping their pupils working unnecessarily long at some little part of the subject, they often weaken their interest in learning the language. Perhaps one should not merely **sprinkle** the pupil, but **plunge** him right down into the sea of language and enable him to swim by himself as soon as possible. A great deal will arrange itself in the brain without the learning of too many special rules or the aid of **elaborate** explanations.

Notes

1. **Otto Jespersen**

   Otto Jespersen (1860–1943), a Danish linguist and a foremost authority on English grammar, was the chair of the English Department at the University of Copenhagen. Among his many works, *Modern English Grammar* and *Analytic Syntax* are very influential.

2. **the sea of language (Line 55)**

   The sea of language refers to the language environment where learners immerse themselves and acquire the language naturally. Metaphor is used here to give readers a vivid impression of the vast environment in which a child learns and acquires his or her mother tongue.

STUDY READING

A Structure Analysis

Fill in each blank with no more than three words according to your understanding of the text.

The comparison between children's learning their mother tongue and adults' learning a foreign language is both (1) _____. The sharp contrast is that children without prior knowledge or professional teachers but oral instruction have a(n) (2) _____ of the native language while adults with fully-developed mental powers, specially-trained language teachers and various learning tools only have a(n) (3) _____ command of the foreign language. I suppose the difference lies both in the (4) _____ and in the behavior of the (5) _____. Specifically, the mother tongue is learned in the first years of life when there is (6) _____. In addition, the child hears the natural language (7) _____ with the right gestures and facial expressions. Finally, people around him make the learning a(n) (8) _____ experience.

B Reading Comprehension

I Sequencing: Identify the order of the following statements according to the text.

_____ A During the early years of life, a child is exposed to a favorable environment in learning his native language.

_____ B Teachers often require that children spend long time on trivial linguistic points, which may lead to children's loss of interest in language learning.

_____ C It is believed that children, compared with grown-ups, have more flexible speech organs.

_____ D Compared with adults, children lack developed mental powers.

_____ E Children make many mistakes while learning a language.

_____ F Nonverbal languages help children understand what they hear.

II Blank Filling: Fill in each blank with no more than three words based on the text.

1. _____ adults' foreign language learning, children are often found to learn mother tongue much better.

2. When a grown-up learns a foreign language, the whole learning task _____ systematically.

3. What _____ the inexact command of a foreign language by a highly gifted grown-up?

4. That children's complete mastery of mother tongue depends on their organs of speech cannot _____.

5. A child's higher language proficiency _____ both the child and the people around him.

6. Gestures and _____ together with the language spoken in any situation contribute a lot to children's language learning.

7. The so-called "teachers" of a child _____ to make their lessons interesting and instructive.

8. Perhaps a more favorable way to children's language learning is to make them _____ the sea of language.

III Group Work: It is generally believed that there are differences between an adult's learning a foreign language and a child's acquisition of his or her mother tongue. What is your opinion? Work in groups and have a discussion. Then you are required to recommend a representative to share your ideas in class.

WORD BUILDING

A Prefabs

Exercise 1 Blank Filling: Active Words

I Study the meanings of the active nouns, verbs and adjectives in the table.

Active Words

3	**comparison** /kəmˈpærɪsn/ *n.*	[C] When you make a comparison, you consider two or more things and discover the differences between them.
12	**visual** /ˈvɪʒuəl/ *adj.*	Visual means relating to sight, or to things that you can see. *music, film, dance, and the visual arts*
18	**flexible** /ˈfleksəbl/ *adj.*	A flexible object or material can be bent easily without breaking. *brushes with long, flexible bristles*
21	**acquire** /əˈkwaɪə(r)/ *vt.* V n	If you acquire something such as a skill or a habit, you learn it, or develop it through your daily life or experience. *to acquire new skills*
25	**detect** /dɪˈtekt/ *vt.* V n	If you detect something, you notice it or sense it, even though it is not very obvious. *to detect a certain sadness in the old man's face*
30	**favorable** /ˈfeɪvərəbl/ *adj.*	Favorable conditions make something more likely to succeed or seem more attractive. *to be too favorable to the government*
44	**attempt** /əˈtempt/ *n.*	[C] If you make an attempt to do something, you try to do it, often without success.
44	**fulfill** /fʊlˈfɪl/ *vt.* V n	If you fulfill something such as a promise, dream, or hope, you do what you said or hoped you would do. *to fulfill one's promise*
49	**awkward** /ˈɔːkwəd/ *adj.*	An awkward movement or position is uncomfortable or clumsy. *to make an awkward gesture*
49	**sympathy** /ˈsɪmpəθi/ *n.*	[U] If you have sympathy with someone's ideas or opinions, you agree with them.
52	**accuracy** /ˈækjərəsi/ *n.*	[U] If someone or something performs a task, for example, hitting a target, with accuracy, they do it in an exact way without making a mistake.

II **Now complete the sentences with the words in the table above. You need to change the form where necessary.**

1 Making these statements that are factually incorrect calls into question the _____ of the entire article.

2 Despite the dim lighting in the engine room, he _____ a faint shadow on the far wall.

3 It takes chimps (黑猩猩) up to four years to _____ the necessary skills to select and adequately use the tools to crack a nut.

4 Those who come to Yoga class learn ways to breathe, stretch and become more _____.

5 Now there is very little to prevent them from making history and advancing beyond a World Cup group at the first _____.

6 There are very strong arguments that wind turbines (风力发动机) spoil the _____ appearance of the landscape.

7 I have some _____ with this point of view on euthanasia in some countries and regions.

8 After college, he tried to _____ his dream of becoming a screenwriter by enrolling in classes at New York University.

9 _____ were made among subgroups of students to examine whether different aspects of memory were important to different kinds of students.

10 People could tell that she faked her clumsy and _____ movements, often purposely stumbling over anything that came her way.

11 People have the right to work in _____ conditions, the right to health and to a healthy environment, and the right to have access to food.

Exercise 2 Prefab Translation

I Discuss the meanings of the following prefabs in the text.

Prefabs

7	mental power	31	what is more important
12	visual aid	33–34	drink in
21–22	with no small difficulty	37	all the year round
27	in sb.'s opinion	43	again and again
31	from morning till night	46–47	take pains

II Translate the following into English, using the prefabs in the table above.

1 培养和扩展学龄前儿童的心智 _____

2 借助直观教具进行课堂教学 _____

3 一例难度不小的脑外科手术 _____

4 依鄙人之见 _____

5 从早到晚地辛勤劳作 _____

6 更为重要的是，产品价廉质优。 _____

7 不断吸收新思想 _____

8 一年四季宜人的气候 _____

9 三番五次地劝某人戒烟 _____

10 下更大的功夫写好毕业论文 _____

B Partial Dictation

Listen to the following sentences once only and fill in the blanks with the exact words you hear.

🎧 6.02

1. Compared with a little child, an adult is a _____.
2. For a grown-up person, teaching task is elaborately _____ in a system.
3. The teaching approach for children is limited to oral instruction; the adults can get access to _____.
4. It is said that a child's _____ is more flexible than an adult's.
5. At the beginning of training, a child can scarcely _____.
6. A child in a native language environment _____ genuine linguistic forms.
7. The child can acquire the language, _____ the matching paralanguage.
8. _____ of language learning, difficulties can become the most pleasant experience by the child.

C Sentence Translation

Translate the Chinese sentences into English, using the expressions in the brackets.

1. 新校区下学期的教学计划都安排好了。(*lay out*)

2. 据说一个人的成功70%取决于情商的高低。(*account for*)

3. 在我看来，他的观点没有一个是站得住脚的。(*hold water*)

4. 矛盾的普遍性寓于矛盾的特殊性之中。(*lie in*)

5. 他的人物画在当时可谓登峰造极。(*as it were*)

Translation Tips

Translating "Organ Words" Properly

The phrase "mother tongue" in the first sentence of the text refers to the language learned by children and passed from one generation to the next, i.e., one's native language, or "母语" in Chinese. In this very context, the word "tongue" does not stand for the fleshy, movable, muscular organ of taste, an aid in chewing and swallowing. Nor can it be translated into "舌头" in Chinese. It will be laughable to translate "mother tongue" into "母亲的舌头". One needs to secure the referential and pragmatic equivalence when translating the "organ words" or organ-related expressions as follows:

- speak with a forked tongue（用分叉的舌头说话 ×）
- bite one's tongue（咬住舌头 ×）
- find one's tongue（找回舌头 ×）
- hold one's tongue（屏住舌头 ×）
- loosen one's tongue（放松舌头 ×）
- lose one's tongue（失去舌头 ×）
- be on the tip of one's tongue（处于某人的舌尖部位 ×）
- a slip of the tongue（舌头打滑 ×）
- have a sweet tooth（长着一颗甜牙 ×）
- count noses（数鼻子 ×）
- pull sb.'s leg（拉住某人的腿 ×）
- pay lip service（尽嘴唇之力 ×）
- smile from ear to ear（从耳朵笑到耳朵 ×）
- see eye to eye（眼对眼地看着 ×）
- see with half an eye（用半个眼睛看 ×）

To translate the examples above properly, a translator is expected to exercise his subjectivity, paying special attention to the pragmatic meaning of the "organ words" in the expressions, respectively:

- speak with a forked tongue（搪塞；撒谎）
- bite one's tongue（保持沉默）
- find one's tongue（能开口了；恢复说话能力）
- hold one's tongue（不开口，缄默）
- loosen one's tongue（信口开河，大放厥词）
- lose one's tongue（语塞，噤不能言）
- be on the tip of one's tongue（话到嘴边）
- a slip of the tongue（说走嘴；失言）
- have a sweet tongue（爱吃甜食）
- count noses（清点人数）
- pull sb.'s leg（开玩笑）
- pay lip service（敷衍；口惠实不至）
- smile from ear to ear（笑得合不拢嘴）
- see eye to eye（看法一致）
- see with half an eye（一望而知，一看就明白）

GRAMMARING

A *however* + adj./adv.

However, when paired with an adj./adv., means roughly the same as "even if very…" or "it doesn't matter how". Note the word order: *however* + adj./adv. + subject + verb. Here are some examples:

- *However rich* those people are, they always want more.
- We are determined to solve this problem, *however long* it takes.

In the following examples, the verb is omitted:

- If you take money from the fund, *however small the amount*, you must record it in this book.
- Here a complete mastery of the language *however stupid the children*.

I Rewrite the underlined parts of the following sentences, using *however*.

1 I'll call you from Tokyo even if it costs much.
_____

2 No matter how hard he tried, he could not control his feelings.
_____

3 It doesn't matter how many times you explain things. You can never get him to understand.
_____

4 Victory at all costs, victory in spite of all terror, victory no matter how long and hard the road may be.
_____

5 Random acts of kindness, even if it may be very small, can transform the world.
_____

6 It doesn't matter how late he is, his mother waits for him to have dinner together.
_____

II Complete the following sentences.

1 They will never be satisfied however _____.

2 I will not eat junk food however _____.

3 You have to sit the exams, however _____.

4 However _____, I can't agree with him on this occasion.

5 We're determined to have a wonderful holiday, however _____.

6 However _____, I could not solve the puzzle.

7 He'll never catch us however _____.

8 However _____, there is always something you can do, and succeed at.

B plural-only nouns

Plural-only nouns are nouns which are used only in plural form, or which, in a given sense, occur only in plural form. Here are some examples.

- Nouns which are used only in plural form:
  clothes, pants, pyjamas, shorts, trousers, jeans, tights, scissors, binoculars, tongs, belongings, earnings, congratulations, outskirts, premises, surroundings, thanks, wages…

- Nouns which are used only in plural form in a particular sense or senses:
  arms (weapon)   *pains* (great care or trouble)
  goods (property)   *minutes* (a record of proceedings)
  spirits (mood)   *brains* (the intellect)
  contents (a list of the chapters or sections given at the front of a book)

Compare the italicized words in the following sentences.

- The *damage* to his reputation was considerable. (damage = loss, harm)
- These *damages* have not yet been paid. (damages = compensation in money imposed by law for causing loss or injury)

I Complete the sentences with the words in the box.

| outskirts | clothes | pains | minutes | thanks | belongings |

1 Make sure your _____ are tagged with your name before you check them in.

2 I want to offer a word of _____ to all those who helped.

3 If your _____ are wet, you can dry them upstairs.

4 The _____ of the city are really pretty and they stretch for miles.

5 They take great _____ to make their lessons easy and interesting.

6 Who is going to take _____ at the meeting this afternoon?

II Choose the appropriate forms in the brackets to complete the sentences.

1 I cannot find my scissors. Have you seen _____ (it, them)?
2 I need a pair of _____ (glass, glasses) to protect my eyes.
3 My trousers _____ (is, are) dirty. I need to wash _____ (it, them).
4 Many _____ (congratulation, congratulations) on your birthday!
5 You should use your _____ (brain, brains).
6 Take down the _____ (particular, particulars) of this event.

COMMUNICATING

A Viewing: Babies' Acquisition of Language

I Get Prepared: Study two screenshots from the video that you are going to watch. Fill in the blanks with the words from the box.

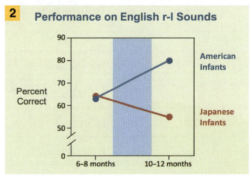

| ten | twelve | discriminate | American | differences |
| eight | English | explained | interesting | similar |

From Picture 1, we can see that there are different distributions of two sound types between the Japanese and (1) _____ languages. English speakers (2) _____ /r/ and /l/ but Japanese speakers do not. Picture 2 indicates that (3) _____ and Japanese babies have (4) _____ performance on r-l sounds during the period from six to (5) _____ months but their performances diverge since then, and there are significant (6) _____ during the period from ten to (7) _____ months, which suggests that something (8) _____ happens during the period from eight to (9) _____ months. This time frame is (10) _____ in what is usually referred to as the hypothesis of the critical period for phonological acquisition.

II Get Prepared: You will hear these proper names and words and expressions in the video. Read aloud the proper names in Table 1. Then study the words and expressions in Table 2.

Table 1	Proper Names
Tokyo	（日本）东京
Seattle	（美国）西雅图
Taipei	（中国）台北
Mandarin	普通话

Unit 6 **Language Learning** (163)

Table 2 Words and Expressions	
pound	击打
discriminate	区分
culture-bound	受文化束缚的
equivalent	同等的
motherese	（与儿童说话时所用的）妈妈语
intently	专心地
bilingual	双语的；双语者
monolingual	单语的；单语者
at once	同时；立即
expose... to...	将……置于……之中
representation	表示，表征
control group	对照组，控制组
dosage	剂量

III Watch and Listen for Gist: Watch the video and complete the sentence with the information you hear.

The speaker mainly talks about what happens to babies during the (1) _____ period from (2) _____ to (3) _____ months for (4) _____ development.

IV Watch and Listen for Gist: Watch ▶6.03 again and put the experiments in the order presented by the speaker.

A A comparison of reactions to Chinese sound changes between American babies exposed to both Chinese and English and Chinese babies exposed to only Chinese.

B A comparison between Chinese and American baby reactions to Chinese sound changes.

C A comparison between American and Japanese baby reactions to English sound changes.

D Reactions of babies to sound changes.

E A comparison between babies exposed to face-to-face sounds and babies exposed to video or audio sounds.

V Watch and Listen for Details: Watch the first episode of the video and sequence the steps in the experiment.

A   A panda bear pounds a drum.

B   Babies react to a sound change by turning their heads.

C   A sound change occurs.

D   Babies sit on parents' laps.

E   Sounds are played.

F   Babies react at an appropriate time.

VI Watch and Listen for Details: Watch the second episode of the video and write down the four questions you hear.

1   _____

2   _____

3   _____

4   _____

VII Watch and Listen for Details: Watch ▶ 6.05 again and choose the correct answers to the questions.

1   What does "a citizen of the world" mean according to the speaker?

   a. A person who is discriminated against because of his or her tongue.

   b. A person who can recognize all sound differences of all languages.

   c. A person who can speak all the languages in the world.

2   What does "a culture-bound listener" mean according to the speaker?

   a. A person who can only distinguish the sounds of his or her mother tongue.

   b. A person who can only speak his or her own language.

   c. A person who is bound to his or her own culture.

3   When does a citizen of the world turn into a culture-bound listener?

   a. From six to eight months.

   b. From eight to ten months.

   c. From ten to twelve months.

VIII **Watch and Listen for Details:** Watch the third episode of the video and complete each of the sentences with the best choice.

1 During the critical period, babies _____.

   a. turn into citizens of the world

   b. absorb sound features of their mother tongue

   c. discriminate sounds of a universal language

2 People become culture-bound listeners when they are _____.

   a. no longer absorbing subtle sound changes

   b. governed by their limited memory

   c. bound by their early development

3 The research findings help us understand that _____.

   a. babies are governed by the representations in memory during the critical period

   b. sound learning distributions change the models of what the critical period is about

   c. the acquisition of language sounds speeds up when their distributions stabilize

IX **Watch and Listen for Details:** Watch ▶6.06 again and fill in the blanks with the three time periods from the box.

> a. From six to eight months   b. From eight to ten months
> c. From ten to twelve months

Task and Results	Period
American babies are exposed to Mandarin.	
Chinese babies perform better than American babies.	
American babies perform the same as Chinese babies.	

X Watch and Listen for Details: Watch the fourth episode of the video and complete each of the sentences with the correct choice.

1. A control group was needed for the experiment because the researcher wanted to know _____.
    a. whether exposure to Chinese environment improves English
    b. whether exposure to English environment improves Chinese
    c. whether exposure to laboratory environment improves Chinese

2. The major finding of the new language exposure experiment is that _____.
    a. American babies can acquire Chinese sounds as well as Chinese babies do
    b. there is no advantage for Chinese babies to learn Chinese
    c. babies will take whatever you put in front of them

3. The last two sentences mean that language acquisition _____.
    a. is controlled by human society
    b. is only found among social animals
    c. cannot take place without real social contacts

XI Watch and Infer Information: Watch ▶ 6.07 again and circle the correct answer to the question.

Which of the following statements will the speaker most likely support?

a. Parents can talk to their babies from six to ten months over phones to learn language.

b. Parents should talk to their babies from eight to ten months as much as they can.

c. All babies around ten to twelve months should start learning a new language.

B Speaking

Activity 1 — Do You Like Learning Languages?

6.08

I Complete the conversation by filling in the blanks with appropriate expressions. Then listen and check your answers.

A: Do you like learning languages?

B: Yes, I do. I love traveling and talking to the local people in their (1) _____.

A: What is your mother tongue?

B: English.

A: What second language are you learning?

B: I'm learning Spanish. I (2) _____ Spanish food and culture when I traveled to Spain three years ago.

A: That's really interesting. Is Spanish popular in your country?

B: Yes. People in my country come from every corner of the world and Spanish is the second popular language spoken there.

A: (3) _____ do you use that language?

B: Quite a lot. I see Spanish people every day in the restaurant, bank or supermarket.

A: How long have you been learning Spanish?

B: Nearly three years. I'm in advanced class now.

A: Who is your teacher?

B: An elderly Spanish woman. She can also speak English fluently.

A: Wow! That's cool. I'm just curious, (4) _____ why do people learn a second language?

B: Well, people do that for different purposes. Some learn it to do business, others learn it for cultural reasons, and (5) _____ just learn it for fun.

II Pair Work: Practice the conversation with a partner.

III Read the useful expressions aloud.

Useful Expressions for Presenting Reasons and Results			
Why do you think ■ learning English is quite important?			*It is well-known that* English is an international language.
Because I believe *Since I think* *As I find that* ■ it is an international language.	*Owing to* *Due to* *Thanks to* ■ its status as an international language	*Hence,* *Thus,* *Therefore,* ■ it is quite important to learn it well.	*As a result,* *On that account,* *For that reason,* ■ learning English is worthwhile.

IV **Pair Work:** Read the questions below. Add your own question for each situation. Then take turns asking and answering the questions with a partner. Use the expressions above to help you.

Your Teacher	Your Best Friend
■ Why is it important to learn programming languages? ■ Why is it necessary to learn a second foreign language? Your question: _____	■ Why do you prefer print reading to online reading? ■ Why do you speak English whenever and wherever you can? Your question: _____

Activity 2 Child Language Development and More

I Read the information about language development in the chart. Add your own findings.

Some Facts About Child Language Development and More
By the end of 6 months, a baby might make gurgling sounds when playing with you or left alone.
By the end of 12 months, a baby might try imitating speech sounds.
By the end of 18 months, a baby might recognize names of familiar people, objects and body parts.
By the end of 24 months, a baby might use simple phrases, such as "more milk".
The relationship between vocabulary knowledge and grey matter density was specific to the teenage years.
Committed language students experience growth in the hippocampus (海马体), a brain region associated with learning and memory, as well as in parts of the cerebral cortex (大脑皮质), or the outmost layer of the brain.
People who use more than one language frequently find themselves having different patterns of thought and reaction as they shift.
Those who speak a second language can delay dementia, e.g., Alzheimer's disease, by as long as 5 years.
Your findings: _____

II **Pair Work:** Use the information in the chart above and discuss language learning. You may use the model dialog for help.

6.09

A: Why should babies be exposed to their first languages at the early stage of their lives?

B: Because there is a critical window of opportunity for the cortical language areas of their brains to be activated.

A: Does this explain why learning a new language is difficult for adults?

B: Not necessarily. Some new studies show that our brains are prepared for changes at different time frames in our life. As a result, you can learn a new language at any time of your life. Where there is a will, there is a way.

A: But it still takes so much time and energy to learn a second language. Why can't I invest these on other things?

B: Well, being bilingual can improve your health and slow down aging effects on your body.

A: You know, some people propose that we do not need to learn a foreign language anymore, thanks to the invention of machine translation devices.

B: That's only partially true, because knowing a foreign language by yourself can enrich your perspective on the world and society and enable you to evaluate the quality of the device.

C Writing

I **Fill in the blanks with phrases from the box to complete the paragraphs. You may need to make necessary changes to some of the phrases.**

mother tongue	lay out	a complete mastery of
in most cases	account for	hold water
detect differences	lie partly in	in the first place
all the year round	visual aid	from morning till night
mental power	take pains	

We all know that one learns (1) _____ with much greater ease than a foreign language. Comparison and experiments tell us that the difference does not consist in intelligence, experience or knowledge of the learner, for less bright children may show (2) _____ the mother tongue while highly intelligent adults find it hard to have a good command of a foreign language even though the task (3) _____ for them, with such necessary assistance as textbooks, professional teachers, etc. Then what (4) _____ the difference?

Many explanations do not (5) _____. One of the erroneous views is that the difference (6) _____ the organ of speech, the child's organ being more flexible than the adult's organ, and partly in the ear, the child's ear being more sensitive than the adult's ear. The fact is that (7) _____ children can produce correct sounds only after numerous mistakes they have made. Their flexibility of the tongue is acquired, with great difficulty. And then children's ear, in the first stage of life, can't (8) _____ in sounds.

The real answer is that children live in the very language environments in the first stage of life, from morning till night, (9) _____, (10) _____ with those dearest and nearest people speaking the language all the time. They are being tutored privately non-stop, thus acquiring by degrees how the native language is appropriately used in different situations to express ideas, thoughts and feelings.

II **Now write an essay of about 220 words on *Language Learning*. You may use the phrases from the box above.**

TEXT B Embracing the Ambiguity

Steward Lee Beck & Katie Lu

embrace *vt.* 欣然接受
ambiguity *n.* 模棱两可的话
crave *vt.* 渴求

point of contention 争论焦点
refuge *n.* 庇护
confrontation *n.* 对抗
understate *vt.* 避重就轻地说
deprive *vt.* 剥夺
unravel *vt.* 揭开，阐明

substance *n.* 要旨，实质

abrupt *adj.* 唐突的
dangle *vt.* （作为诱惑物）炫示

embody *vt.* 体现

Westerners **crave** specificity and directness; they like getting to the point. Easterners prefer the indirect approach, talking around **points of contention**, seeking **refuge** in ambiguity to avoid **confrontation**, and **understating** themselves wherever possible.

5　　Chinese would much rather *rao quanzi* (beat about the bush) than let on you're about to make a strategic error which could cost your company millions. Why **deprive** others of the pleasure of **unraveling** the hidden meaning behind their carefully chosen words?

10　　The thinking goes something like this: Time is of no consequence as long as I'm filling up these moments with words, often without saying anything of **substance**. After all, not everything need be said between friends, and to reveal my true intentions is far too **abrupt** and shallow. So please, relax, be
15　patient, and perhaps, eventually… I'll **dangle** a clue about what I really want. And don't worry, if you miss the first dangling, I'll dangle again later.

　　If you are *hanxu* (humble, subtle) and able to **embody** and contain this depth, you are considered well-educated with refined
20　tastes. In terms of inner substance, the more you show, the less you have.

　　The culturally Chinese mind considers *ti yaoqiu* (asking for things) and *you xuqiu* (needing things) as too direct, even rude. There's also a preference for leaving room for correction,
25　so someone might say *keneng ba* (maybe) to a dinner invitation just to keep his options open. If he later chooses to go, he can tell the hostess that he has time. If he decides at the last minute

not to go, and an upset hostess is still holding a seat for him, he can fall back on his original "maybe". In other words, rudeness is **subjective** and ambiguity in China **equates** to flexibility and saving face.

Here are two delicious ambiguities you may encounter in China:

Hen nanshuo

Translation: It's hard to say.

True meaning: I have no idea; or I know and don't want to say.

An elegant way to **dodge** any question or **curtail** any inquiry. Like its cousin *shuobuding* (can't say for sure), the possible reasons why she isn't saying are infinite. So if you're on a date and this phrase pops up, it could mean you're approaching the promised land. Or, you failed to read between the lines and you'**re toast**—date over.

Yihou zaishuo

Translation: Let's talk about it later.

True meaning: I'm hoping we'll both forget and it never comes up again.

Not disagreement, not agreement, not agreeing to disagree. It's a temporary **deferment** that might not be revisited. This phrase most often comes up when the speaker is…

(a) **acknowledging** the complexity of a situation and its many variables, or

(b) preventing you from raising a sensitive topic in front of clients, or

(c) clueless on the subject and doesn't want others to know.

It's up to you to figure out whether you're with a sensitive genius or a clever **ignoramus**.

No discussion on Chinese ambiguity would be complete without talking about the *Dao*, the Chinese "way of being" attributed to the philosopher Laozi who lived around 550 B.C. during the Spring and Autumn Period. The *Dao* accounts for the long, poetic love affair the Chinese people have with ambiguity.

The opening **verse** from the *Daodejing* (*The Classic of*

---

subjective *adj.* 主观的
equate *vi.* 等同

dodge *vt.* 躲开
curtail *vt.* 限制

be toast 完蛋，遭殃（非正式）

deferment *n.* 拖延

acknowledge *vt.* 承认

ignoramus *n.* 无知的人

verse *n.* 诗节

transient *adj.* 短小精悍的
sublime *adj.* 绝妙的
mysticism *n.* 神秘主义

invoke *vt.* 唤起，引起
caution *vi.* 告诫
elevate *vt.* 抬高（地位）
obsession *n.* 痴迷
duality *n.* 二元性
suppress *vt.* 压制
backfire *vi.* 适得其反
mystifying *adj.* 令人困惑的

annoy *vt.* 惹恼

reef *n.* 暗礁
rip *vt.* 撕裂
shred *n.* 碎片

the Virtue of the Dao) by Laozi sets the stage for 81 **transient** passages exploring the **sublime mysticism** of life:

The Way that can be expressed is not the everlasting Way. Names that can be named are not changeless names.

Daoists believe that in the perfectly balanced universe, the existence of a quality **invokes** its opposite. They **caution** against our human tendency to **elevate** one quality and reject its opposite, such as when a person's **obsession** over beauty leads to feeling ugly. In a world of **dualities**, high and low, light and dark, good and evil, it's impossible to eliminate one without the other. Even attempts to **suppress** a quality you want to eliminate can **backfire**; in other words, the more laws, the more thieves.

China can be frustrating from time to time and **mystifying** to both newcomers and old China hands alike. But as foreigners, we all know that coming in. What could be more foolish than to continue to live somewhere and complain nonstop about it? There are ten thousand things here to **annoy** you, and a million things here to make you happy. It's your choice.

Where there is opportunity, there is challenge in a sea of ambiguity. Fortunately for us, surfing the wave of ambiguity is easy to learn. It's a balancing act of flowing with your surroundings, while ignoring the **reef** that can **rip** you to **shreds**.

Notes

1. **Steward Lee Beck & Katie Lu**
   Steward Lee Beck is an American who has conducted business in China since the early 1990s, with experiences in high-tech, financial services and charitable events. Katie Lu is a native Chinese who runs PITT Services (translation and training) and EnglishPlus (children's English learning). They collaborated on the book *China Simplified: Language Empowerment* (2019).

2. ***Dao* (Taoism) (Line 59)**
   Dao is a Chinese philosophy based on the writings of Laozi, speaking highly of humility and religious piety. Philosophical Taoism advocates inner contemplation and mystical union with nature.

EXERCISES

A Reading for Gist

Answer the following questions according to your understanding of the text.

1. What's the difference between Westerners and Easterners according to the authors?

   _____

   _____

2. How do you understand this sentence: "Why deprive others of the pleasure of unraveling the hidden meaning behind their carefully chosen words?"

   _____

   _____

B Reading for Details

Each of the following statements contains information given in the text. Identify and write down the corresponding number of the paragraph from which the information is derived.

1. For Chinese people, going straight to the point is considered inappropriate; instead, giving clues is preferred. Para. _____

2. People who are humble and indirect are considered well-educated. Para. _____

3. *Dao* is a necessary component that makes the discussion of Chinese ambiguity complete. Para. _____

4. In the world, every substance coexists with its opposite and both parts are indispensable. Para. _____

5. Learning the practice of ambiguity helps you better balance your relations with the surrounding environment. Para. _____

C Reading Beyond

Talk in small groups about other cultural conflicts in different cultural contexts and how to overcome them.

Unit 6 **Language Learning**

D Prefabs

Write the Chinese meanings of the following prefabs in the text.

get to the point _____

deprive sb. of sth. _____

of no consequence _____

leave room for… _____

hold a seat _____

save face _____

set the stage _____

beat about the bush _____

hidden meaning _____

refined taste _____

at the last minute _____

fall back on… _____

read between the lines _____

old China hand _____

E Sentence Translation

I Translate the English sentences into Chinese.

1 Easterners prefer the indirect approach, talking around points of contention, seeking refuge in ambiguity to avoid confrontation, and understating themselves wherever possible.

2 In a world of dualities, high and low, light and dark, good and evil, it's impossible to eliminate one without the other.

3 It's a balancing act of flowing with your surroundings, while ignoring the reef that can rip you to shreds.

II Translate the Chinese sentences into English, using the expressions in the brackets.

1 请直说吧，不要拐弯抹角的。(*get to the point*)

2 现在大概是傍晚六点钟。(*something like*)

3 安排工作时，我们应该为不可预见的情况留有余地。(*leave room for*)

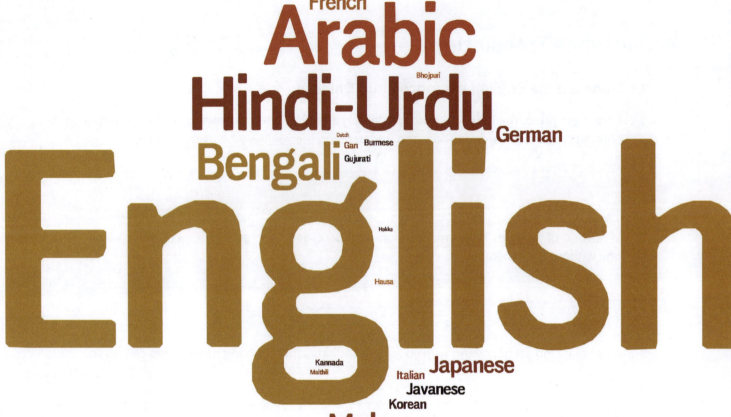

Unit 7 Reading

Warming Up

Memorize and comment on the following quotations on reading.

1. 凡读书，须要读得字字响亮，不可误一字，不可少一字，不可多一字，不可倒一字。不可牵强暗记，只是要多诵遍数，自然上口，久远不忘。

   ——朱熹

2. To learn to read is to light a fire; every syllable that is spelled out is a spark.

   — Victor Hugo

INITIAL READING

A Vocabulary

Read the new words aloud and try to work out their meanings in the text.

New Words

5 **blurred** /blɜːd/ *adj.*
7 **biography** /baɪˈɒgrəfi/ *n.*
7 **flattering** /ˈflætərɪŋ/ *adj.*
8 **banish** /ˈbænɪʃ/ *vt.*
9 **preconception** /ˌpriːkənˈsepʃn/ *n.*
11 **dictate** /dɪkˈteɪt/ *vi.*
12 **accomplice** /əˈkʌmplɪs/ *n.*
16 **imperceptible** /ˌɪmpəˈseptəbl/ *adj.*
18 **steep** /stiːp/ *vt.*
24 **impalpable** /ɪmˈpælpəbl/ *adj.*
33 **comic** /ˈkɒmɪk/ *adj.*
34 **conception** /kənˈsepʃn/ *n.*

34 **contained** /kənˈteɪnd/ *adj.*
37 **subdue** /səbˈdjuː/ *vt.*
44 **trudge** /trʌdʒ/ *vt.*
48 **accustom** /əˈkʌstəm/ *vt.*
51 **moor** /mʊə(r)/ *n.*
52 **uppermost** /ˈʌpəməʊst/ *adj.*
52 **solitude** /ˈsɒlətjuːd/ *n.*
57 **strain** /streɪn/ *n.*
60 **wrench** /rentʃ/ *vt.*
61 **uproot** /ˌʌpˈruːt/ *vt.*
62 **finesse** /fɪˈnes/ *n.*
63 **boldness** /ˈbəʊldnəs/ *n.*

B Skimming

Read Text A and go through the statements within eight minutes. Circle the numbers of the correct statements.

1 It's easy for us to get what we truly need from books since they can be divided into different categories.

2 It would be a good start for us to get rid of the prejudgments about what the books should be like when we read.

3 If you hesitate to read and make comments at the beginning, you will gain no value from the book.

4 Keep your mind open, and you will get into a unique world with indefinite possibilities.

5 Reading can help us totally understand what the writer has conveyed in a novel.

6 To write clearly what has impressed you might be a tough process.

7 Different authors share the same understanding of artistic conception in literary works.

8 Great novelists keep consistency in their writing.

9 The author employs simile in the last paragraph to show how challenging it is to read a novel.

10 Keen insight and rich imagination are required to fully understand and grasp the essence of a novel.

TEXT A — How to Read

Virginia Woolf

It is simple enough to say that since books have classes—fiction, biography, poetry—we should separate them and take from each what it is right that each should give us.

Yet few people ask from books what books can give us. Most commonly we come to books with **blurred** and divided minds, asking of fiction that it shall be true, of poetry that it shall be false, of **biography** that it shall be **flattering**, of history that it shall enforce our own prejudices. If we could **banish** all such **preconceptions** when we read, that would be an admirable beginning.

Do not **dictate** to your author; try to become him. Be his fellow-worker and **accomplice**. If you hang back, and reserve and criticize at first, you are preventing yourself from getting the fullest possible value from what you read.

But if you open your mind as widely as possible, then signs and hints of almost **imperceptible** fineness, from the twist and turn of the first sentences, will bring you into the presence of a human being unlike any other. **Steep** yourself in this, acquaint yourself with this, and soon you will find that your author is giving you, or attempting to give you, something far more definite.

The thirty-two chapters of a novel—if we consider how to read a novel first—are an attempt to make something as formed and controlled as a building: But words are more **impalpable** than bricks; reading is a longer and more complicated process than seeing. Perhaps the quickest way to understand the elements of what a novelist is doing is not to read, but to write; to make your own experiment with the dangers and difficulties of words.

Recall, then, some event that has left a distinct impression on you—how at the corner of the street, perhaps, you passed two people talking. A tree shook; an electric light danced; the tone of the talk was **comic**, but also tragic; a whole vision, an entire **conception**, seemed **contained** in that moment.

But when you attempt to reconstruct it in words, you will find that it breaks into a thousand conflicting impressions. Some must be **subdued**; others emphasized; in the process you will lose, probably all grasp upon the emotion itself.

Then turn from your blurred and littered pages to the opening pages of some great novelist—Defoe, Jane Austen, Hardy. Now you will be better able to appreciate their mastery. It is not merely that we are in the presence of a different person—Defoe, Jane Austen, or Thomas Hardy—but that we are living in a different world.

Here, in *Robinson Crusoe*, we are **trudging** a plain high road; one thing happens after another; the fact and the order of the fact is enough. But if the open air and adventure mean everything to Defoe, they mean nothing to Jane Austen. Hers is the drawing room, and people talking, and by the many mirrors of their talk revealing their characters. And if, when we have **accustomed** ourselves to the drawing room and its reflections, we turn to Hardy, we are once more spun around.

The **moors** are round us and the stars above our heads. The other side of the mind is now exposed—the dark side that comes **uppermost** in **solitude**, not the light side that shows in company. Our relations are not towards people, but towards nature and destiny.

Yet different as these worlds are, each is consistent with itself. The maker of each is careful to observe the laws of his own perspective, and however great a **strain** they may put upon us they will never confuse us, as lesser writers so frequently do, by introducing two different kinds of reality into the same book.

Thus to go from one great novelist to another—from Jane Austen to Hardy, from Peakcok to Trollope, from Scott to Meredith—is to be **wrenched** and **uprooted**; to be thrown this way and then that. To read a novel is a difficult and complex art. You must be capable not only of great **finesse** of perception, but of great **boldness** of imagination if you are going to make use of all that the novelist— the great artist—gives you.

Notes

1. **Virginia Woolf**
   Virginia Woolf (1882–1941), original name in full Adeline Virginia Stephen, was a British female writer, literary critic, and theorist, as well as representative of stream of consciousness literature in the 20th century. Best known as the author of *Mrs. Dalloway* and *To the Lighthouse*, she was also a prolific writer of essays, diaries, letters, and biographies.

2. **Defoe (Line 40)**
   Daniel Defoe (1660–1731) was an English novelist, pamphleteer, and journalist. Labelled as a social historian for his

interest in colonization, economics, and exploration, he is best known for *Robinson Crusoe* and *Moll Flanders*.

3. **Jane Austen (Line 40)**
   Jane Austen (1775–1817) was an English writer in the Georgian era who first gave the novel its distinctly modern character through her treatment of ordinary people in everyday life. She is best known for her social commentary in novels including *Sense and Sensibility*, *Pride and Prejudice*, *Mansfield Park*, and *Emma*.

4. **Hardy (Line 40)**
   Thomas Hardy (1840–1928) was an English novelist and poet. As a novelist he is best known for his work set in the semi-fictionalized county of Wessex including *Far from the Madding Crowd*, *The Return of the Native*, *Tess of the D'Urbervilles*, and *Jude the Obscure*.

5. **Peakcok (Line 60)**
   Thomas Love Peakcok (1785–1866), an English novelist and poet, was the most distinctive prose satirist of the Romantic period. *Nightmare Abbey* is his best-known work in which romantic melancholy is satirized.

6. **Trollope (Line 60)**
   Anthony Trollope (1815–1882), an English novelist and postal worker in the Victoria era, is best known for his serial novels, *Chronicles of Barsetshire*. *The Warden* is the first and the best of the series.

7. **Scott (Line 60)**
   Walter Scott (1771–1832), a Scottish novelist, poet, historian and biographer, is considered both the inventor and the greatest practitioner of the historical novel. *Waverley*, his first novel, was published anonymously and its worldwide success prompted further volumes in the *Waverley* series.

8. **Meredith (Line 60)**
   George Meredith (1828–1909) was an English Victorian poet, essayist, and novelist. His novels are characterized by their wit, brilliant dialogs, and aphoristic quality of language. *The Ordeal of Richard Feverel* and *The Egoist* are his best-known works.

STUDY READING

A Structure Analysis

Fill in each blank with no more than three words according to your understanding of the text.

To read a novel is a difficult and (1) _____ art. It would be an admirable beginning if we could (2) _____ as widely as possible and banish our (3) _____ when we read. Imperceptible fineness will bring us into the presence of a human being. And soon we will find that the author is giving us something far more (4) _____. It is not merely that we are in the presence of a different person—but that we are living in a different (5) _____. However different these worlds are, each is consistent with itself. Our relations with the novel are not towards people, but towards (6) _____. We must be capable not only of great (7) _____, but of great (8) _____.

B Reading Comprehension

I Sequencing: Identify the order of the following statements according to the text.

_____ A Readers should abandon their preconceptions before reading.

_____ B Opening your mind and getting absorbed in reading help you understand the author better.

_____ C Presenting different worlds for readers, writers are consistent with themselves in some way.

_____ D Books can be divided into such categories as fiction, biography, poetry and others.

_____ E It is difficult to depict memorable scenes in words even if they impressed you.

_____ F Readers often expect history books to coincide with their prejudiced ideas.

II Blank Filling: Fill in each blank with no more than three words based on the text.

1 If you want to benefit most from what you read, don't _____ and rush to judgements from the outset.

2 When you immerse yourself in the book and _____ the book, you'll find that the author tries to convey something far more definite.

3 Before you start writing, you might as well recollect the event that has _____ on you.

4 The environment and incidents in Defoe's novel may _____ Jane Austen.

5   When people _____ the settings and characters of Jane Austen's novel, those of Hardy's will probably confuse them.

6   In Hardy's works, people's dark side _____ is revealed instead of the brilliant side in company.

7   Although the worlds created by different novelists are quite different, each is _____ itself internally.

8   Both delicate perception and bold imagination can help you _____ what the great novelist attempts to deliver.

III **Group Work:** How do you understand the sentence "Do not dictate to your author; try to become him." in Para. 3? Work in groups and have a discussion. Then you are required to recommend a representative to share your ideas in class.

WORD BUILDING

A Prefabs

Exercise 1   Blank Filling: Active Words

I Study the meanings of the active nouns, verbs and adjectives in the table.

Active Words

8	**enforce** /ɪnˈfɔːs/ *vt.* V n	To enforce something means to force or cause it to be done or to happen. *to enforce a low-tech specification*
8	**prejudice** /ˈpredʒədɪs/ *n.*	[C] Prejudice is an unreasonable dislike of a particular group of people or things, or a preference for one group of people or things over another.
18	**acquaint** /əˈkweɪnt/ *vt.* V n *with* n	If you acquaint yourself with something, you learn about it. *to acquaint yourself with your strengths and weaknesses*
21	**definite** /ˈdefɪnət/ *adj.*	Definite evidence or information is true, rather than being someone's opinion or guess. *definite proof*
27	**element** /ˈelɪmənt/ *n.*	[C] The different elements of something are the different parts it contains.
30	**distinct** /dɪˈstɪŋkt/ *adj.*	If something is distinct, you can hear, see, or taste it clearly. *a distinct flavor*
33	**tragic** /ˈtrædʒɪk/ *adj.*	A tragic event or situation is extremely sad, usually because it involves death or suffering. *a tragic accident*
33	**vision** /ˈvɪʒn/ *n.*	[C] If you have a vision of someone in a particular situation, you imagine him or her in that situation.
48	**reveal** /rɪˈviːl/ *vt.* V n	To reveal something means to make people aware of it. *to reveal the whereabouts of her daughter*
49	**reflection** /rɪˈflekʃn/ *n.*	[C] Your reflections are your thoughts about a particular subject.
54	**destiny** /ˈdestəni/ *n.*	[U] Destiny is the force which some people believe controls the things that happen to you in your life.
56	**perspective** /pəˈspektɪv/ *n.*	[C] A particular perspective is a particular way of thinking about something, especially one that is influenced by your beliefs and experiences.
57	**confuse** /kənˈfjuːz/ *vt.* V n	To confuse someone means to make it difficult for him or her to know exactly what is happening or what to do. *to confuse him*
62	**perception** /pəˈsepʃn/ *n.*	[U] Someone who has perception realizes or notices things that are not obvious.

II **Now complete the sentences with the words in the table above. You need to change the form where necessary.**

1 When you don't have a primary-care doctor to coordinate your care, no one has a complete _____ of your health but you.

2 If you check into a big hotel, you might be _____ who to tip—the person bringing the bags from your car, the person bringing them to the reception, or the staff bringing the bags to your hotel room.

3 The reformer is certain to be applauded if successful, because his object is _____ and clear to everyone.

4 The twins not only looked exactly alike, but also talked identically with only subtlest differences in their choice of words, which did not escape Miss Jerram's keen _____.

5 As always when she approached the beautiful stone house, she detected the _____ smell of roses in the air, although she could see no blooms in the courtyard.

6 Opinions, thoughts and _____ I wrote in my blog are all personal. Readers are strongly advised not to draw any conclusion whatsoever on the basis of my write-ups.

7 He does it because he enjoys taking it upon himself to _____ thin privilege.

8 One of the key _____ in his report was a shift in emphasis from heavy to light industry in an effort to improve supplies of consumer goods.

9 Remember, you don't know what you don't know, so you want to be very critical about your own _____ as well, instead of reacting defensively to critiques.

10 This views a disabled person as limited more by society's _____ than by the actual disability.

11 The existence of the lobby (游说) is a political fact; and before we can get rid of it, we must _____ ourselves with its causes.

12 When the economy was bad, the papers reported nearly every day the _____ ending of the life story of men who had lost their "savings" and who felt that they could no longer live.

13 Cautiously and tenderly as the truth was _____ to her, she became dizzy and pale, with the suddenness of the shock.

14 "Heaven knows," said he, "what will become of me, or where my _____ will lead me. I am a leaf the wind blows on his unsteady currents."

Unit 7 **Reading** (187)

Exercise 2   Prefab Translation

I Discuss the meanings of the following prefabs in the text.

Prefabs

6	ask of	49	turn to
12	hang back	49–50	spin around
16–17	twist and turn	53	in company
18	steep oneself in	55	be consistent with
48	accustom oneself to	57	put a strain upon

II Translate the following into English, using the prefabs in the table above.

1 求人不如求己 _____

2 面对困难绝不退缩 _____

3 迂回曲折的改革过程 _____

4 沉浸在节日的气氛中 _____

5 难以适应一线城市的生活方式 _____

6 遇到困难及时向邻居求助 _____

7 旋转几圈后感觉头昏眼花 _____

8 和朋友们一起在河里游泳 _____

9 始终与党中央保持一致 _____

10 避免给考生增加额外的压力 _____

B Partial Dictation

Listen to the following sentences once only and fill in the blanks with the exact words you hear.

1 Books can be _____ fiction, biography, poetry and so on, and the readers can take in nutrition from reading.

2 The ideal beginning of reading is to remove _____ held by common people.

3 While reading, criticism or bias will prevent readers from getting _____ from the books.

4 If you open your mind, you can notice subtle language use and _____.

5 When you describe the event in words, it will be _____ to reproduce the vivid scene.

6 When reading the masterpieces of _____, you are living in that time.

7 Jane Austen's works are focused on the living room where different characters _____ through conversations.

8 When we are around the moors and stars written by Hardy, the dark side of human nature in solitude _____.

C Sentence Translation

Translate the Chinese sentences into English, using the expressions in the brackets.

1 对别人敞开心扉是结交好友的第一步。(*open one's mind*)

2 要使你自己熟悉一项新工作是需要时间的。(*acquaint… with*)

3 没有主题的谈话绝不会给人留下鲜明的印象。(*leave an impression on*)

4 简言之，一个人应该知晓自己的实力，不要试图去做远远超越自己能力的事情。(*attempt to*)

5 听了这一番话后，我的脑海顿时出现了一大片空白。(*break into*)

Translation Tips

From "Fellow-Worker" to "Migrant Worker" and the Like

In Para. 3 of the text, one of the sentences reads: "Be his fellow-worker and accomplice." One may translate the underlined word "fellow-worker" into "同事", "同仁", "同伴", or "工友". By and large, the word "fellow-worker", commonly spelt as "fellow worker", refers to a colleague, a co-worker, a workfellow, who joins with others in some activity or endeavor.

Loosely, this word may remind us of some other synonyms or near synonyms in Chinese, such as "农民工" and "打工人".

The former came into being after the 1990s, meaning that rural people, while farming, went out to help others in their spare time. With the growing need for the urban development of cities, some of them simply put down their hoes and come to the cities to work, hence the term "农民工" and its English translations, say, "migrant worker", "off-farm worker", or "rural laborer".

The latter, an online hot word sought after by young people from all walks of life, is a general term for workers who engage in physical labor or are technically skilled. With making money as their first and sometimes only goal, they are a resolute group, who would rarely be caught arriving late to work or leaving early. They can be all kinds of employees, from blue-collar workers and low-level staff to managers. Taking into account such contextual and pragmatic meanings, we may as well render the term "打工人" into "laborer", "commuter", or "wage earner".

GRAMMARING

A *as*: with special word order to express concession

In formal style, we use *as* to mean "though" in "adj./adv./n. + *as* + S + V" construction. This construction suggests a very emphatic contrast. For example:

- Smart *as* he is, he will just never get the joke.

    (= Although he is very smart, he will just never get the joke.)

- Much *as* I'd like to stay, I really must leave now.

    (= Though I'd very much like to stay, I really must leave now.)

- Child *as* he is, John can understand three foreign languages.

    (= Though he is only a child, John can understand three foreign languages.)

Though is also possible in this construction. For example:

- Bravely *though* they fought, they had no chance of winning.
- Genius *though* she was, she was quite unassuming.

> - We do not use *although* in this construction.
> - We can use *that* in this construction in British English. For example:
>   - Poor *that* they were, they gave money to charity.
> - In American English, *that* is used after a noun phrase. For example:
>   - Fool *that* he was, he managed to evade his pursuers.

I Rewrite the underlined parts of the following sentences, using the "adj./adv. + *as*" pattern.

1   <u>Though I'm hungry</u>, I will not eat anything now.

    _____

2   <u>Although it was cold</u>, we went out.

    _____

3   <u>Although I was very tired</u>, I went on working.

    _____

4   <u>Although I had enjoyed my adventure very much</u>, it was good to be back.

    _____

5   Although these worlds are very different, each is consistent with itself.

   _____

6   Though I'd very much like to see Paris some day, I'm pretty content to stay right here in my hometown for the time being.

   _____

7   Though their survival seemed miraculous, it was nothing to what lay ahead.

   _____

8   Though it may be incredible, there is no college in such a big city.

   _____

II Fill in the blanks to complete the sentences.

_____ as _____,
- he came to work.
- don't give up.
- I cannot agree with him on the issue.
- he knows a lot about the ecosystem.
- the students enjoy reading it.

B directive + *and/or*...

When the first clause in the "clause + *and/or* + clause" pattern is a directive, it serves as the condition of the second clause. For example:

- Take my advice *and* your troubles will be over.

   (= If you take my advice, your troubles will be over.)

- Ask me no questions, *and* I'll tell you no lies.

   (= If you ask me no questions, I'll tell you no lies.)

Note that *or* implies a negative condition. For example:

- Start at once, *or* you'll miss the train.

   (= If you don't start at once, you'll miss the train.)

I Rewrite the following sentences, using the "directive + and/or…" pattern.

1   If you give him an inch, he'll take a mile.
   _____

2   If you tidy up your room, you can go out to play football with your friends.
   _____

3   If you don't keep to the path, you will lose your way.
   _____

4   If you stick to your principles, you will win through.
   _____

5   If you acquaint yourself with this, soon you will find that your author is giving you something far more definite.
   _____

6   If you don't start immediately, you won't be able to finish the work as scheduled.
   _____

II Add a clause to each of the following sentences.

Work hard,
Think it over,   and   _____.
Try again,

Study harder,
Be quiet,   or   _____.
Hurry up,

COMMUNICATING

A Viewing: Old Reading Habits

I Get Prepared: Complete the chart below. Read and explain your answers to a partner.

My favorite book	
My bad reading habits	
My good reading habits	
My average reading speed	_____ words per minute

II Get Prepared: You will hear these words and expressions in the video. Read them aloud.

Words and Expressions	
fixation / fixate (on)	死盯着；过于关注
on a word-by-word basis	逐字地
syllable	音节
peak one's interest	使人产生浓厚兴趣
regression	回看
subvocalization	默读
recap	扼要重述

III Watch and Listen for Gist: Watch the video and choose the best title for the talk.

a. It is easy to improve our reading skills.
b. We should change three bad reading habits.
c. Techniques and exercises can help us read faster.

▶ 7.03

IV Watch and Listen for Details: Watch ▶7.03 again and fill in the blanks in the chart with the information you hear.

Habit	What It Means	Why You Do It	Why It Is Bad
Fixation	Your eyes (1) _____ while reading.	You are not fully capable of reading (2) _____, so you have to (3) _____ syllable by syllable.	(4) _____

(Continued)

Habit	What It Means	Why You Do It	Why It Is Bad
Regression	You (5) _____ _____ while reading.	It is an issue with (6) _____ _____	
Subvocalization	You (7) _____ _____ _____ while reading.	It is common among all readers.	

V Watch and Infer Information: Watch part of the video and circle the correct answer to the question.

▶ 7.04

Which of the statements is true based on what the speaker says?

a. We're less likely to re-read the material if it is interesting enough.

b. It is common that we read a whole page and then stop to think.

c. Usually people do not re-read dry and dull books.

VI Watch and Listen for Language Use: Watch part of the video and fill in the blanks with the exact words you hear.

▶ 7.05

You don't have to say a word in your head to know what it means. For example, when you're driving a car and you see a stop sign, do you say "stop" in your head? Probably not. You don't have to say the word "stop" in your head to know (1) _____. But if the word "stop" was in the middle of some paragraph you were reading, you probably would say "stop" in your head and (2) _____ with subvocalization. (3) _____ we need to change this old reading habit (4) _____ it slows us down. Think about it. If you're saying every word in your head, doesn't that mean you'll only read as fast as you talk? And (5) _____.

The average reading speed is 150 to 250 words a minute. Guess what the average talking speed is? (6) _____ it's exactly the same, 150 to 250 words a minute. Why is the average reading speed the same as the average talking speed? (7) _____ this habit subvocalization. If you say every word in your head while reading, then you'll only (8) _____, and (9) _____. Subvocalization limits our reading speed.

B Speaking

Activity 1 Reading Is Important.

I Complete the speech by filling in the blanks with appropriate expressions. Then listen and check your answers. 🎧 7.06

(1) _____ the importance of reading.

(2) _____ why I'd like to talk about reading.

(3) _____ I think are important for reading.

(4) _____ the reason why I choose this topic. This is mainly due to what I find in my neighborhood. I noticed that people used to read a lot twenty years ago. Now they spend so much time on their mobile phones. They don't read any more. And this is not right. I think it is important that people read books.

(5) _____ that books are the main sources from which we can get new knowledge and wisdom about nature and the human society. They can open your mind. When you read great books, you'll find yourself in the presence of men of wisdom. There's a lot you can learn from them.

(6) _____ that through reading you can make friends with other people. You can share books with others and by doing this you may find that you both experience similar or even the same kind of feelings or emotions and understanding of life. Reading is like a bridge. Sometimes, you can even make friends with great authors.

(7) _____, reading is a great way to educate yourself to be an independent person with a good personality, great perseverance, and self-confidence. The most important thing in life, I think, is our concentration. We are now living in a different world. We need to get rid of all the distractions around us and keep moving on; we need to get rid of all the harassment of WeChat and insist on studying attentively. We're never going to succeed if we waste our time on mobile phones.

II **Pair Work:** Practice the speech in front of your partner.

III Read the useful expressions aloud.

Useful Expressions for Giving Presentations	
Stating the Purpose	Stating Important Points
■ Today, I'd like to talk to you about… ■ I'll begin by talking about… ■ I'll provide an overview of… ■ Then I'll list the (two/three/four) things/reasons…	■ Let's talk first about… ■ Let's start by talking about… ■ One of the main reasons for… / causes of… is… ■ Another/A second reason for… / cause of… is… ■ And finally…

IV **Pair Work:** Read the information below. Add your own preference. Then make a short speech on what books you read in one of the situations and explain your choice to your partner. Use the expressions above to help you.

Books	Situations
Detective stories Love stories Science fiction Biographies and autobiographies Children's books Politics and economics Military and world affairs Food, travel, sports and culture	1. Books to read with friends
	2. Books to read on the train
	3. Books to read on the bed
	4. Books to read on the Internet
Your preference: _____	Your preference: _____

Activity 2   How Much Do You Read?

I Read the information in the chart. Add your own time for each situation.

Reading Time in the Library	Reading Time in the Classroom
An hour a day Two hours a day Four hours a day Your time: _____	An hour a day Two hours a day Three hours a day Your time: _____
Reading Time While Doing Chores	**Reading Time in the Dorm**
Half an hour a day An hour a day Your time: _____	An hour a day Two hours a day Your time: _____

II **Pair Work:** Use the information in the chart above and discuss how much you read every day. You may use the model dialog for help.

7.07

A: Reading is an important part of my life. I read for two hours every day.

B: Really? How do you find time to read so much?

A: It's a combination of several factors. First of all, it's due to audiobooks. These make up at least a third of my reading in the past few years. I read, or to be more precise, listen to books while commuting, working out, washing dishes, and doing other chores. Over an hour a day spent on all these combined is not uncommon.

B: How marvelous!

A: Besides, I find that I can read books together with my roommate that both of us actually enjoy. This is just like audiobooks in a way—it allows me to "steal" reading time while doing something else. Reading together with my best friend is a lot of fun, and it combines an activity that's dear to my heart with another activity—reading.

B: That's true. Book-lovers keep company with each other.

A: Most important of all, I make time. I find that I have some free time almost every evening to relax; it's usually not much, maybe 30 minutes. Rather than watching TV or browsing social media, I read. Each instance in isolation is not much, but it really adds up over time.

B: Yes. You're truly an incredible reader! I think there's a lot that I can learn from you.

C Writing

I Fill in the blanks with phrases from the box to complete the paragraphs. You may need to make necessary changes to some of the phrases.

hang back	open one's mind	twist and turn
acquaint oneself with sth.	leave an impression on sb.	it is not merely that
in the presence of	open air	accustom oneself to sth.
the other side of the mind	the dark side	be capable of sth.

    Before we read, we should not (1) _____ but just (2) _____ sufficiently wide and get prepared to face what will be revealed to us, no matter how strange or even shocking it might be.

    While we are reading, great events, surprising (3) _____ in a certain story, a perfect melody, a splendid imagination, and a lofty moral purity may (4) _____, thus (5) _____ something spiritually wonderful. Sometimes, we feel charmed. (6) _____ we are (7) _____ a certain writer, but because we are immersed in an enchanting world the writer has created. Sometimes, (8) _____ or (9) _____ is exposed, as we are reading some stories about the dark aberrations of the human spirit and the activated evil in human words and deeds as if we are going through a long dark tunnel. When we see how good prevails over evil in the end, we are beginning to see the great light at the end of the dark tunnel. By the time we (10) _____ ups and downs and wheels within wheels, after reading tons of books about history, novels and the like, we are sufficiently sophisticated to understand diversity and complexity of life.

II Now write an essay of about 220 words on *How to Read*. You may use the phrases from the box above.

TEXT B Sweet Potato Porridge

Lin Mei

recline *vi.* 斜倚	
rim *n.* 边缘	
dismal *adj.* 悲伤绝望的；糟糕的	
tulip *n.* 郁金香	
hydrangea *n.* 绣球花	
fragrance *n.* 香气	
pervade *vt.* 弥漫	
nutritious *adj.* 有营养的	
ginseng *n.* 人参	
esculent *adj.* 可食用的	
vexed *adj.* 烦恼的	
wither *vi.* 凋谢	
tonic *n.* 滋补品	
toil *vi.* 劳累，苦干	
unfilial *adj.* 不孝顺的	
frown *vi.* 皱眉	
tablet *n.* 药片	
amicably *adv.* 友善地	

The ward was quiet. Lao Kong was **reclining** on the bed with his eyes closed. The **rims** of his eyes went black and those dark and thick eyebrows held out with all their might. He was in such a **dismal** situation. After just one month in hospital, he lost one third of the weight.

On the bedside table, **tulips**, roses, **hydrangeas** and other flowers the visitors brought to him gave off waves of **fragrance** which **pervaded** the whole room. The cabinet was filled with various **nutritious** food, such as **ginseng**, **esculent** swift's nest, essence of chicken… However, Lao Kong was not happy at all. He felt **vexed** very much. Hundreds of Belgian Francs for a bunch of flowers! They would **wither** in two or three days. It was really a waste of money. Besides, he had no appetite for so many **tonics**.

In the year when he retired, he came to Europe from China. After twenty years, he still couldn't get used to the life here. Yesterday, at dusk, he said to his son, "Send me home."

The son comforted him, "You **toiled** for the whole life, and now you'd better enjoy your late life here; besides, I am a boss and if I send you back home I will be considered **unfilial**. When mother was alive, I was still poor, but now…"

Lao Kong **frowned** and said, "The Chinese herbal medicine is better."

At this time, the female nurse came in and the son had to leave.

Moving his body a little, Lao Kong took the **tablet** from the nurse and held it in hand. For fear that he might throw the tablet away as he did yesterday, the nurse hurriedly handed him a cup of warm water and said to him **amicably**, "You'll recover sooner or later."

"I know I've got a fatal disease. What's the point of concealing the fact from me? It usually happens in this age…" He said to the nurse with the tone full of contempt and tolerance toward death. Turning his head and licking his dry lips, he said, "Please do me a favor. Call my daughter-in-law and tell her I want to eat nothing but sweet potato porridge."

The nurse lowered her voice and said, "But…but it's hard to buy sweet potatoes here!"

The old man nodded. A mist of disappointment and regret turned up in his eyes.

These days, he had a poorer appetite. Every day, his son specially asked someone to send him cooked food—abalone, sea cucumber and shark's fin, for fear that he might be lack of nutrition. However, the only thing he desired was his hometown flavor—the sweet potato porridge, which he ate every day in his childhood and teenage.

He was old, and always lingered in the past. They were very vivid and clear in his memory. As a matter of fact, he hadn't eaten sweet potato porridge for tens of years, but now he was eager for it.

He was born in a small village in the southeast coast of China. The yellow soil in his hometown was so poor that only sweet potatoes could grow. Local people had two crops of sweet potatoes per year, and when the potatoes were ripe they cut some potatoes into pieces with a planer tool and aired them under the sun. When the potatoes got dried, people put them into wooden pails. Thus, the main food for the whole year was preserved. Other potatoes were just scattered in random on the ground covered with lime, and people could boil them at any time.

Sweet potatoes could be cooked in various ways, such as roasting or boiling, and the most popular way was boiling them together with rice. The porridge made by them was so sweet, glutinous and delicious that one can eat it up without any dishes.

Nevertheless, sweet potato porridge was mainly for the poor at that time.

Now, where to buy sweet potatoes? The son got worried.

To satisfy the old man's wish, his daughter-in-law asked about it everywhere. Their friends and relatives had been here for several years or even tens of years, but they still kept in touch with their relatives in the hometown and they always had some

---

conceal *vt.* 隐藏

abalone *n.* 鲍鱼
fin *n.* 鳍

linger *vi.* 徘徊

planer *n.* 刨子

random *n.* 随意
lime *n.* 石灰

glutinous *adj.* 黏的

pickle n. 腌菜
shrimp n. 虾
anticipate vt. 预料

native special products in store, such as **pickles**, dried fish or small **shrimps**. Maybe someone had sweet potatoes?

As **anticipated**, Lao Liu kept some sweet potatoes in his home.

The daughter-in-law boiled the dried sweet potatoes together with a little rice. The yellowish red potato slices in the porridge tasted as sweet, smooth and glutinous as fresh sweet potatoes.

In the evening, the daughter-in-law sent the porridge to the hospital. The old man was very excited. He erected his body, thanked her, and had two bowls of porridge.

At 3 o'clock that night, the nurse could not wake him up.

He departed peacefully, with a smile on his face.

Notes

1. **Lin Mei**

   Lin Mei (1985–) is a Chinese-American chef and television personality and best known as the winner of the twelfth season of the Bravo television network's reality television series, *Top Chef*. In 2019, she opened her first restaurant, Nightshade in Los Angeles. In 2020, Nightshade was named a James Beard Foundation Award finalist for Best New Restaurant.

2. **Chinese herbal medicine (Line 21)**

   Also known as Traditional Chinese Medicine (TCM), Chinese herbal medicine uses various mind and body practices such as acupuncture (针灸), Guasha treatment, and tai chi, as well as herbal products to address health problems. They may help improve quality of life and certain pain conditions.

EXERCISES

A Reading for Gist

Answer the following questions according to your understanding of Text B.

1 How is Lao Kong's homesickness embodied in the text?

   _____
   _____

2 Lao Kong's shifts of emotions towards the sweet potato porridge are vividly described in the story. Could you please highlight these descriptions?

   _____
   _____
   _____

B Reading for Details

Decide whether the following statements are true (T) or false (F).

1 Lao Kong couldn't get used to the life in Europe so many years after his retirement. T F

2 Lao Kong lost one third of his weight after being bedridden for months in the hospital. T F

3 Lao Kong wanted very much to go back home to try Chinese herbal medicine because he didn't want to die. T F

4 Lao Kong desired his hometown flavor—the sweet potato porridge because he missed home so much. T F

5 Lao Kong's daughter-in-law was filial because she tried every means to satisfy his last wish. T F

6 Lao Kong died in peace with a smile on his face probably because of the euthanasia (安乐死). T F

C Reading Beyond

I **Read the following quote of Lao Kong's son and share your understanding with your classmates.**

"You toiled for the whole life, and now you'd better enjoy your late life here; besides, I am a boss and if I send you back home I will be considered unfilial."

Unit 7 **Reading** 203

II "When mother was alive, I was still poor, but now…" What was omitted? Please use your imagination and finish the words of the son.

D Prefabs

Write the Chinese meanings of the following prefabs in the text.

essence of chicken _____

at dusk _____

Chinese herbal medicine _____

what's the point of doing…? _____

as a matter of fact _____

have no appetite for _____

enjoy one's late life _____

for fear that _____

a mist of _____

satisfy sb.'s wish _____

E Sentence Translation

I Translate the English sentences into Chinese.

1 The son comforted him, "You toiled for the whole life, and now you'd better enjoy your late life here; besides, I am a boss and if I send you back home I will be considered unfilial. When mother was alive, I was still poor, but now…"

_____

_____

2 Local people had two crops of sweet potatoes per year, and when the potatoes were ripe they cut some potatoes into pieces with a planer tool and aired them under the sun.

_____

_____

3   The yellowish red potato slices in the porridge tasted as sweet, smooth and glutinous as fresh sweet potatoes.

II **Translate the Chinese sentences into English, using the expressions in the brackets.**

1   天一黑，市中心的路灯就都亮了。(*at dusk*)

2   我怎么也没想到拼命干活反倒落了一身不是。(*nothing but*)

3   本表所有排名不分先后。(*in random*)

Unit 8 Generosity

Warming Up

Memorize and comment on the following quotations on generosity.

1 君子贵人贱己，先人而后己。

— 《礼记》

2 That's what I consider true generosity. You give your all, and yet you always feel as if it costs you nothing.

— Simone de Beauvoir

INITIAL READING

A Vocabulary

Read the new words aloud and try to work out their meanings in the text.

New Words

Title	generosity /ˌdʒenəˈrɒsəti/ n.	31	afterlife /ˈɑːftəlaɪf/ n.
2	outward /ˈaʊtwəd/ adj.	31	appease /əˈpiːz/ vt.
2	underlying /ˌʌndəˈlaɪɪŋ/ adj.	31	conscience /ˈkɒnʃəns/ n.
2	motive /ˈməʊtɪv/ n.	33	ultimate /ˈʌltɪmət/ adj.
15	fault /fɔːlt/ vt.	36	altruistic /ˌæltruˈɪstɪk/ adj.
15	praiseworthy /ˈpreɪzwɜːði/ adj.	36	wellbeing /ˈwelˈbiːɪŋ/ n.
19	attachment /əˈtætʃmənt/ n.	37	donor /ˈdəʊnə(r)/ n.
24	philanthropy /fɪˈlænθrəpi/ n.	46	empathy /ˈempəθi/ n.
25	motivate /ˈməʊtɪveɪt/ vt.	58	blameworthy /ˈbleɪmwɜːði/ adj.
26	publicity /pʌˈblɪsəti/ n.	58	withhold /wɪðˈhəʊld/ vt.
30	deduction /dɪˈdʌkʃn/ n.		

B Skimming

Read Text A and go through the statements within eight minutes. Circle the numbers of the correct statements.

1. This text is mainly about what qualities generous people should possess.
2. It is easy to tell whether one is generous or not.
3. Actions speak louder than words when we define whether one is generous or not.
4. Jones' donation is not generous because what he donates is of no value to him.
5. Amanda cares about not only praise and fame but also the welfare of others.
6. What Amanda has done truly contributes to a better world.
7. The author uses subjunctive mood to illustrate that generosity does exist.
8. There's a correlation between altruistic motivation and people's attitude towards others.
9. Professor Smith's behavior is praiseworthy but not generous, because he is just fulfilling his duty.
10. The author uses different examples to illustrate the requirements for being generous.

TEXT A — True Generosity Involves More than Just Giving

Christian B. Miller

Virtues such as generosity are complicated. They involve more than just **outward** behaviour. A person's **underlying** thoughts, feelings and **motives** matter, too. If those aren't in good shape, then one cannot qualify as a generous person.

So what more is involved in being a generous person besides consistently donating one's money, time and resources? I want to propose three requirements we have to meet to qualify as generous people. Needless to say, there are others, but I find these to be particularly interesting and controversial.

First comes donating something of value to you. Consider the following example:

Jones has completely lost interest in the CDs in his car; he hasn't played them in years, and they are just gathering dust. One day, he happens to drive by a Goodwill collection centre, and decides that it would be nice to get rid of them. So he drops them off.

I don't want to **fault** what Jones did. It is **praiseworthy**, and Goodwill can put the donation to good use. But is his donation generous? I am inclined to say no. If Jones had still been attached to the CDs and thought that donating them could do some good in the world, then that would be one thing. But he lost all **attachment** to them years ago. When acting generously, a person gives something of value to him, something that he cares about, even if only to a small degree.

Next up is not focusing on oneself. Here is another example:

Amanda has been donating to various charities for a number of years, and today she is receiving a community award for her **philanthropy**. Although she doesn't tell this to other people, what has **motivated** her to make these donations has always been the **publicity** and recognition.

Again, we can agree that the world is a better place because Amanda has donated so many times. Thank goodness she helped people over the years, rather than not. Yet here too we don't find an expression of generosity. The same is true if her motivation had been to earn tax **deductions**, to get rewards in the **afterlife** or to **appease** a guilty **conscience**. What all these have in common is that they are self-focused. The person who donates her money or time for these reasons is **ultimately** concerned only about herself, and not those who would be helped by the donation.

So a second requirement is that a generous person's motives in donating have to be primarily **altruistic**, or concerned with the **wellbeing** of those who would be helped, regardless of whether the **donor** will benefit in the process. If she does, that's great! But if she doesn't, that's OK, too. Her benefit is not the point. Note that I said "primarily". Some self-interested reasons could be present, too. But the altruistic motives had better be stronger.

If this is on the right track, it raises a challenging question about the very existence of generosity. For suppose there is no such thing as altruistic motivation, perhaps everything we do aims only at our self-interest. Then it would follow that there is no generosity either.

Fortunately, research in psychology suggests otherwise. We have good reason to think that altruistic motivation exists. Interestingly, though, as far as we can tell, this happens in only one way—through **empathy**. If you empathise with, say, other people's suffering, you are more likely to help them, and there is a good chance that your motivation will be altruistic.

So generosity survives, but it seems to first require an empathetic state of mind. That's why the third and final requirement I want to mention here is going above and beyond. This can be illustrated with the following example:

Professor Smith has just finished meeting with a student about her paper. As the student leaves, she says: "Thank you for making the time to meet with me." Smith replies, in a completely serious tone of voice: "Don't worry about it. I'm just doing my job. Professors are required to meet with students if office hours are not compatible with their schedules. See you tomorrow in class." He then shuts the door.

Again, admirable of him to meet with her, I would say. But not generous.

Generous acts are gifts. And gifts are never required. They are freely given, and never **blameworthy** if **withheld**. Hence to act from a heart of generosity, we give when (and only when!) we think we have the moral freedom to do so. We go above and beyond the call of duty.

Notes

1. **Christian B. Miller**

   Christian B. Miller is a productive professor at Wake Forest University, North Carolina, U.S.A. His research is primarily in contemporary ethics and philosophy of religion, and much of his current research is at the intersection of philosophy and psychology.

2. **Goodwill (Line 13)**

   Goodwill is an American nonprofit organization that provides job training, employment placement services and other community-based programs for people who have barriers preventing them from obtaining a job. It is funded by a massive network of retail thrift stores which operate as nonprofit as well.

STUDY READING

A Structure Analysis

Fill in each blank with no more than three words according to your understanding of the text.

True generosity is complicated. It involves (1) _____ just giving. A person's underlying thoughts, feelings and motives matter, too. To qualify as generous people, we have to meet (2) _____ requirements. First comes donating something (3) _____ to you. When acting generously, a person gives something that he cares about, even if only to a small extent. A second requirement is that a generous person's motives in donating have to be primarily (4) _____, or concerned with the (5) _____ of those on the receiving end. The third and final requirement is going above and beyond the call of (6) _____. Generous acts are gifts that are (7) _____ given, and never required or (8) _____ if withheld.

B Reading Comprehension

I Sequencing: Identify the order of the following statements according to the text.

_____ A If people donate something valuable to themselves, we say they are truly generous.

_____ B People helping others mainly out of altruistic motives are generous.

_____ C The meaning of generosity is far beyond outward behavior.

_____ D Research findings in psychology indicate that altruistic motivation does exist.

_____ E According to the author, a man has to meet three requirements to be qualified as a generous one.

_____ F If people help others beyond the call of duty, they are generous.

II Blank Filling: Fill in each blank with no more than three words based on the text.

1 What else _____ being a generous person in addition to giving others money, time and resources?

2 _____, other interesting and controversial requirements are needed for one to be qualified as a generous person besides those aforementioned.

3 The dust on the CDs in the car shows that Jones has _____ them.

4 The author _____ say that Jones' donation is not generous.

Unit 8 Generosity (211)

5   Being self-focused is the characteristic that charitable behaviors have _____, such as donating with the purpose of reducing tax, being rewarded in the afterlife and alleviating a sense of guilt.

6   Altruistic behavior means that a person concerns more about the benefits of other people, _____ his own wellbeing.

7   If everything we do _____ our own interest, there would be no true generosity at all.

8   When a person _____ others' suffering, there probably exists altruistic motivation.

III **Group Work: The author proposes three requirements for being generous, namely donating something valuable, being altruistic and going beyond one's duty. Work in groups and make comments on the author's opinion. Then you are required to recommend a representative to share your ideas in class.**

WORD BUILDING

A Prefabs

Exercise 1   Blank Filling: Active Words

I   Study the meanings of the active nouns, verbs and adjectives in the table.

Active Words

1	**complicated** /ˈkɒmplɪkeɪtɪd/ *adj.*	If you say that something is complicated, you mean it has so many parts or aspects that it is difficult to understand or deal with. *a very complicated voting system*
3	**qualify** /ˈkwɒlɪfaɪ/ *vt.* V n *as* n	To qualify as something or to be qualified as something means to have all the features that are needed to be that thing. *to qualify them as experts*
4	**generous** /ˈdʒenərəs/ *adj.*	A generous person gives more of something, especially money, than is usual or expected. *to be generous in lending*
5	**consistent** /kənˈsɪstənt/ *adj.*	Someone who is consistent always behaves in the same way. *his consistent support of free trade*
6	**propose** /prəˈpəʊz/ *vt.* V n	If you propose something such as a plan or an idea, you suggest it for people to think about and decide upon. *to propose changes to some institutions*
8	**controversial** /ˌkɒntrəˈvɜːʃl/ *adj.*	If you describe something or someone as controversial, you mean that they are the subject of intense public argument, disagreement, or disapproval. *a controversial issue*
17	**incline** /ɪnˈklaɪn/ *vi.* V *to* v	If you incline to think or act in a particular way, you are likely to think or act in that way. *to incline to blame the world for their failure*
17	**attach** /əˈtætʃ/ *vt.* be Ved *to* n	If you are attached to someone or something, you like them very much. *to be very attached to her family and friends*
23	**charity** /ˈtʃærəti/ *n.*	[C] A charity is an organization which raises money in order to help people who are sick or very poor, or who have a disability.
50	**illustrate** /ˈɪləstreɪt/ *vt.* V n	If you use an example, story, or diagram to illustrate a point, you use it to show that what you are saying is true or to make your meaning clearer. *to illustrate this difficult point*
54	**compatible** /kəmˈpætəbl/ *adj.* Adj *with* n	If things, for example systems, ideas, and beliefs, are compatible, they work well together or can exist together successfully. *to be compatible with traditions*

II **Now complete the sentences with the words in the table above. You need to change the form where necessary.**

1 The package is offered with two versions: One comes with a USB charging cable that is _____ with any computer or standard USB power adapter, and the other comes with the cable and a wall charger adapter.

2 You may not be _____ to agree, but points of view other than your own do have merit, too.

3 In her book, Postrel offers diverse examples and stories to _____ her concepts.

4 It gets more _____ when countries with different cultures and values are included in the discussion.

5 The project has become highly _____ due to the history and sensitivity of the site.

6 Heselden was also one of Britain's richest and most _____ men. During his life, he donated about $36 million.

7 It is found that the average person makes cash donations to _____ in the range of 2 to 2.75 percent of their adjusted gross income.

8 Research has demonstrated that healthy relationships that provide _____ support to a child's development lead to better social, emotional and cognitive development.

9 Even if I didn't think books _____ as art, I would still enjoy them, and I would still benefit from reading them.

10 One hypothesis (假设) _____ about Steve Jobs' success is that Mr. Jobs' slowness is the key to Apple's success—his focus on the device, his emphasis on perfecting the user experience, meant holding back, not overreaching.

11 Although he does not feel _____ to his mother, moving to a different city and starting a new life is a tough decision.

Exercise 2 Prefab Translation

I Discuss the meaning of the following prefabs in the text.

Prefabs

3	in good shape	25–26	make a donation
7	needless to say	29–30	the same is true
14	drop… off	41	on the right track
16	put… to good use	52	make the time
17	be attached to	59	go above and beyond

II Translate the following into English, using the prefabs in the table above.

1 一辆完好无损的旧车　　　　　＿＿＿＿＿＿＿＿＿＿＿＿＿＿＿＿＿＿＿

2 行走都不行，何况奔跑呢　　　＿＿＿＿＿＿＿＿＿＿＿＿＿＿＿＿＿＿＿

3 开车把这些衬衫送到干洗店　　＿＿＿＿＿＿＿＿＿＿＿＿＿＿＿＿＿＿＿

4 施展本领，干好工作　　　　　＿＿＿＿＿＿＿＿＿＿＿＿＿＿＿＿＿＿＿

5 念念不忘在家乡度过的美好时光　＿＿＿＿＿＿＿＿＿＿＿＿＿＿＿＿＿＿

6 向非营利组织慷慨捐赠　　　　＿＿＿＿＿＿＿＿＿＿＿＿＿＿＿＿＿＿＿

7 反之亦然。　　　　　　　　　＿＿＿＿＿＿＿＿＿＿＿＿＿＿＿＿＿＿＿

8 推动国民经济走上正道　　　　＿＿＿＿＿＿＿＿＿＿＿＿＿＿＿＿＿＿＿

9 力争超越行业要求　　　　　　＿＿＿＿＿＿＿＿＿＿＿＿＿＿＿＿＿＿＿

10 下班后腾出时间看望某人　　　＿＿＿＿＿＿＿＿＿＿＿＿＿＿＿＿＿＿＿

Unit 8 Generosity

B Partial Dictation

Listen to the following sentences once only and fill in the blanks with the exact words you hear.

1. If a person conforms to the three criteria the author put forward, he or she can _____ someone generous.

2. I want to emphasize that there are other requirements for generosity, but the three are very _____.

3. If Jones _____ the CDs and still donated them, he would be a generous person.

4. We cannot _____ of generosity in Amanda's donation.

5. Amanda's donation aims to reduce the tax, to _____ or to pacify a guilty conscience.

6. A generous person _____ altruism, not self-interest.

7. Since generosity is a gift, people should _____ do generous deeds.

8. You do not _____ for refusing to give because generosity is about giving freely.

C Sentence Translation

Translate the Chinese sentences into English, using the expressions in the brackets.

1. 即使每隔几天打扫一次，屋子还是很快就会积灰。(*gather dust*)

2. 数据显示，未来一周内石油和黄金价格将呈现双双走高的趋势。(*be inclined to*)

3. 在乡村度几天假对你会大有好处的。(*do good*)

4. 对这样的提议应作具体评价而不是一概否决。(*rather than*)

5. 我对你的状况表示同情，但我帮不上忙。(*empathise with*)

Translation Tips

The Word "Matter" Matters a Lot

One of the sentences in Para. 1 of the text reads: "A person's underlying thoughts, feelings and motives matter, too." The underlined word "matter" in this context means being of consequence or importance, or carrying weight. When used as a verb, the word "matter" is open to diverse translations in Chinese, including "有关系", "要紧", "重要". Please note the various translations for the word "matter" in the sentences below:

- That's the only thing that matters. (那是唯一重要的事。)

- It matters a lot to the little girl whether we go together or separately. (我们一起去还是分头去，对那个小女孩来说很要紧。)

- The eyewitness' opinions matter greatly in this lawsuit. (在这起诉讼中，目击证人的意见很有分量。)

- Every second matters in healing the wounded and rescuing the dying. (救死扶伤，分秒必争。)

- In my humble position, my words don't matter much; so they won't listen to me anyway. (鄙人身轻言微，他们不会听的。)

- The editorial points out that political work matters in reform and opening up. (社论指出，改革开放一定要讲政治。)

The examples above tell us that the word "matter" matters a lot. So, one needs to cope with the verb "matter" in day-to-day translation at his own discretion. All this helps to achieve the desired communicative effect for the dynamic equivalence in translation.

GRAMMARING

A past perfect

The past perfect is constructed with "*had* + *-ed* participle". We use the past perfect to talk about "past in the past", i.e., an earlier past situation or activity. See the following example:

- Sam had studied Chinese for two years before he came to China.

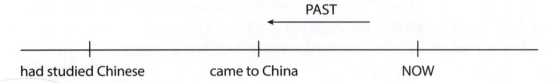

Compare the following sentences:

- When I arrived, Tom *had gone* home.

  (= Tom went home before I arrived.)

- When I arrived, Tom *went* home.

  (= Tom went home after I arrived.)

I Fill in the blanks with the appropriate form of the verbs given in the brackets to complete the sentences.

1. I was informed that the parcel _____ (arrive) the day before yesterday.
2. Mary recalled that they _____ (meet) somewhere before.
3. After she _____ (finish) her degree, she returned to her hometown.
4. I didn't know who she was. I had never _____ (see) her before.
5. At first I thought I _____ (do) the right thing, but I soon realized that I _____ (make) a serious mistake.
6. By the time John _____ (start) his job, we had already _____ (finish) ours.

II Complete the paragraphs with the appropriate verb forms.

1. I thought my train left at 14:33, and _____ (be) very disappointed when I _____ (arrive) at 14:30 and _____ (learn) that it had just _____ (leave). I found later that I _____ (use) an out-of-date timetable.

2. Do you by any chance know where Bob is? I last _____ (see) him about a month ago, when he had just _____ (leave) his job with the film company. He said he was going to France for a holiday and _____ (promise) to send me a postcard with his French address as soon as he _____ (find) a place to stay. But I _____ (hear) nothing since then.

B Type 3 conditional

We use Type 3 conditional to talk about an unreal past condition and its probable past result. In Type 3 conditional, we use past perfect in the conditional clause and "past modal + have done" in the main clause. For example:

- If she *had driven* carefully, she *wouldn't have had* an accident.
- If it *hadn't been* for Margaret, I *might not have understood*.

Compare the four conditional types:

Conditional Type	*If*-clause	Main Clause	Usage	Examples
Zero type	present	present	real condition + inevitable result	If we *turn* to Hardy, we *are* once more spun around.
Type 1	present	*will/can/may* + do	possible condition + probable result	If the London airport *is* clear of fog, we'*ll land* there.
Type 2	past	*would/could/ might* + do	hypothetical condition + possible result	If we *worked* all night, we *would finish* in time; but we have no intention of working all night.
Type 3	past perfect	*would/could/ might* + have done	hypothetical past condition + possible past result	She *might have achieved* greater progress, if we *had given* her more chances.

When we talk about an unreal past condition and its probable result in the present, we use "*had* + *-ed* participle" in the conditional clause and "*would/could/might* + do" in the main clause. For example:

- If you *had listened* to me, you *wouldn't be* in such trouble now.
- If Jones *had* still *been attached* to the CDs, then that *would be* one thing.

I Fill in the blanks with the appropriate form of the verbs given in the brackets to complete the sentences.

1. If you _____ (come), you could have stayed with us.

2. If I _____ (know), I certainly would have helped.

3. If you _____ (work) harder, you would have passed your exam.

4. **A:** How did you do in the car rally?

   B: We came in last actually; but only because we got lost. If we _____ (not get) lost, we _____ (come) in somewhere in the middle. We certainly _____ (not be) last.

5. I am not at all worried about the situation. If I _____ (be) worried, I would not be playing golf at this moment.

6   Be careful about the time. If you _____ (spend) too long on the first question, you _____ (not have) enough time to do the others properly.

II Complete the sentences according to the given situations.

1   Situation: He didn't tell me that he was a vegetarian till halfway through the meal.
    If he _____.

2   Situation: I didn't see the signal, so I didn't stop.
    If I _____.

3   Situation: We didn't visit the museum because we hadn't time.
    If we _____.

4   Situation: It took us a long time to find his house because the streets were not clearly marked.
    If _____.

5   Situation: The launching of the rocket was delayed half an hour by bad weather.
    If _____.

6   Situation: As it took you so much time to get dressed, we haven't arrived at the cinema yet.
    If _____.

COMMUNICATING

A Viewing: Extraordinary Altruists

I **Get Prepared:** Read the passage and fill in the blanks with the words or phrases from the box.

| take off | deceased | normal | removed | transplanting | gives up |

Kidney donation is a practice in which a functioning kidney is (1) _____ from someone and placed into the body of a person who is very ill or dying from organ failure. The donor kidney will function like a (2) _____ kidney once the body has adjusted, allowing the recipient to potentially lead a very healthy, active life.

There are two types of kidney donation: cadaver donation, in which the donor kidney is removed from someone who has (3) _____, and living-donor kidney donation, in which someone (4) _____ a kidney for someone else.

The practice of (5) _____ organs was believed to be theoretically possible for centuries, but it didn't really (6) _____ until the 20th century, when advancements in medical technology made the practice safer and more reliable.

II **Get Prepared:** You will hear these proper names and words and expressions in the video. Read aloud the proper names in Table 1. Then study the words and expressions in Table 2.

Table 1	Proper Names
amygdala	扁桃核（脑部组织名）
St. Augustine	人名
Steven Pinker	人名

Unit 8 **Generosity** 221

Table 2 Words and Expressions	
undergo major surgery	接受大手术
altruist	利他主义者，无私者
detect	觉察，发觉
(under)reactive	（没）有反应的
psychopathic	精神变态的
anchor	锚定，固定
caring continuum	关怀连续体
compassionate	富有同情心的
identify with	认同，有共鸣感，有共同之处
way beyond	远远超出
a telling answer	有力的回答，最能说明问题的回答
inherently	内在地，生来就有地
humility	谦逊，谦恭
at the societal level	在社会层面，从社会角度来看
capital punishment	死刑
ludicrous	可笑的，荒唐的
bone marrow	骨髓
paradoxical	自相矛盾的

III Watch and Listen for Gist: Watch the video and circle the correct answers.

1 An extraordinary altruist may be someone who donates his or her own kidney to _____.

   a. a complete stranger

   b. an acquaintance

   c. his or her lover

2 The main reason why extraordinary altruists are so different is that _____.

   a. they are not so compassionate

   b. they are not self-centered at all

   c. they are not inherently special

3   According to the speaker, most people _____.

   a. are more compassionate than cruel

   b. will become wealthier and better off

   c. can be altruistic and compassionate

IV   Watch and Listen for Details: Watch the first part of the video and decide whether the following statements are true (T) or false (F).

1   Kidney donors can easily detect other people's suffering and fear.   T   F

2   Psychopathic people's amygdalas are underreactive to others' fear.   T   F

3   Extraordinary altruists' amygdalas are 18% larger than average.   T   F

4   There are very psychopathic people and very altruistic people in this world.   T   F

5   Truly extraordinary altruists are compassionate towards all people.   T   F

6   A complete stranger saved the speaker's life some time ago.   T   F

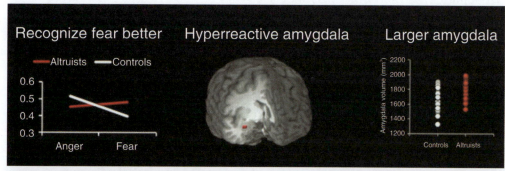

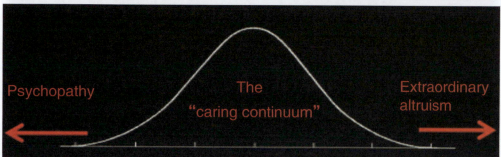

V Watch and Listen for Details: Watch the second part of the video and fill in the blanks with the information you hear. ▶ 8.05

1 It's difficult for altruists to explain why they are willing to _____
   _____.

2 Fewer than _____ Americans have given a kidney to a stranger.

3 True altruists don't think they are _____
   _____.

VI Watch and Listen for Details: Watch the third part of the video and choose the correct answers to the questions. ▶ 8.06

1 Which of the following pictures best describes an extraordinary altruist?

a.   b.   c.

2 What makes men and women as angels?

   a. Their self-centeredness.

   b. Their humility.

   c. Their words.

3 What really distinguishes extraordinary altruists from the average persons?

   a. Total lack of self-centeredness.

   b. Somebody in their inner rings.

   c. Somebody in their outer rings.

4 Why is there more altruism and less cruelty now than before?

   a. Our society is accepting a view of the world that most people are kind.

   b. Psychologists have shown that people fear punishment for cruelty.

   c. People are now less tolerant of others' suffering.

5 What may future people think of kidney donation to a stranger?

   a. It is ludicrous.

   b. It is normal.

   c. It is unacceptable.

VII Watch and Listen for Language Use: Watch the final part of the video and fill in the blanks with the exact words you hear.

▶ 8.07

So what's (1) _____ all these amazing changes? (2) _____ it seems to be increases in wealth and (3) _____. As societies become wealthier and (4) _____, people seem to turn their focus of attention outward, and (5) _____, all kinds of altruism towards strangers increases, from volunteering to charitable donations and even altruistic kidney donations. But all of these changes also (6) _____, which is that even as the world is becoming a better and more humane place, (7) _____, there's a very common perception that it's becoming worse and more cruel, (8) _____. And I don't know exactly why this is, but I think it may be that we now just know (9) _____ about the suffering of strangers in distant places, and so we now care a lot more about the suffering of those distant strangers. But (10) _____ the kinds of changes we're seeing show that the roots of altruism and compassion are (11) _____ a part of human nature (12) _____ cruelty and violence, maybe (13) _____, and while some people (14) _____ inherently more sensitive to the suffering of distant others, I really believe that the ability to (15) _____ and expand the circle of compassion outward to include even strangers is (16) _____ for almost everyone.

B Speaking

Activity 1　Let's Talk About Compassion.

I Complete the speech by filling in the blanks with appropriate expressions. Then listen and check your answers.　🎧 8.08

　　Compassion is (1) _____ a feeling of pity, sympathy, and understanding for someone who is suffering. It implies an urgent desire to aid or help. So it (2) _____ both an understanding of another person's pain and the desire to somehow relieve that pain. In many cases, compassion refers to both a feeling and the action that (3) _____ that feeling.

　　Compassion is not (4) _____ empathy or altruism, though the concepts are related. (5) _____ empathy refers more generally to the ability to (6) _____ and feel the emotions of another person, compassion is when those feelings and thoughts include the desire to help. Altruism, (7) _____, is the kind and selfless behavior often prompted by feelings of compassion, though one can feel compassion without acting on it, and altruism isn't always motivated by compassion.

　　Cynics may (8) _____ compassion as irrational, but scientists have started to map the biological basis of compassion, suggesting its deep evolutionary purpose. (9) _____ that when we feel compassion, our heart rate slows down, and regions of the brain linked to empathy, caregiving, and feelings of pleasure light up, which often results in our wanting to approach and care for other people.

　　As our society is becoming wealthier and better off, an increasing number of people are more compassionate than ever, offering help to those who are in need. This will benefit both the helpers and the helped, and in the long run, the society (10) _____.

II Pair Work: Practice the speech in front of your partner.

III Read the useful expressions aloud.

Useful Expressions for Avoiding the Word *Very*			
Instead of Saying	**Say**	**Instead of Saying**	**Say**
very accurate	exact	*very* nervous	apprehensive
very afraid	terrified	*very* powerful	compelling
very beautiful	gorgeous	*very* smart	intelligent
very cute	adorable	*very* stupid	idiotic
very colorful	vibrant	*very* tired	exhausted
very creative	innovative	*very* ugly	hideous
very evil	wicked	*very* upset	distraught
very glad	overjoyed	*very* valuable	precious
very good	excellent	*very* willing	eager
very necessary	essential	*very* worried	distressed

IV Pair Work: Do you think you are a compassionate person? Share with your partner your understanding of yourself.

Do you think you are a compassionate person?

Yes. I am, to a certain extent. I'm quite rational, normally. But I'll be distraught if I know someone is suffering.

I'm a sensitive person. Seeing people suffering makes me distressed. I'm eager to give them a hand as long as I can.

You're definitely a kind man.

Activity 2 What Will You Do with Things You Do Not Need Anymore?

I Listed in the chart may be things you no longer need. Add your own item for each category.

Things at School				Things at Home				
textbooks	computer	pens	paper	clothes	toys	books	desk	tea
blanket	clothes	bags	flask	chair	bed	bowls	cups	coffee
skateboard	bicycle	cell phone		TV set	umbrella	shoes	towels	
Your item: _____				Your item: _____				

II **Group Work:** Use the information in the chart above and discuss with your partners what you will do with things you do not use anymore. You may use the model dialog for help.

8.09

A: How will you deal with clothes and shoes that you will not wear any longer?

B: I don't know. It's always my mum who handles these things. Personally, I'd just throw them away into the dustbin.

C: I'd give my cast-offs to people in the neighborhood who need them.

B: How do you know if there is anyone who is in need of them?

C: I'd ask people working in the community for the neighborhood committee, and give all these things to them. They will help me find the right people.

A: That's great.

C Writing

I Fill in the blanks with phrases from the box to complete the paragraphs. You may need to make necessary changes to some of the phrases.

in good shape	qualify as	meet the requirements of
needless to say	lose interest in	put sth. to good use
be inclined to do	be attached to sb.	to a small degree
receive an award for	motivate sb. to do	the same is true
have… in common	be concerned with	on the right track
raise a question about	there is a good chance of doing	state of mind
go above and beyond	be compatible with	do good to sb./sth.

Generosity is a virtue so much extolled that everyone wishes to have. But it is in actuality a virtue too complicated for the average man to cultivate with ease. How can one (1) _____ a generous man?

First of all, being a generous man (2) _____ apparently generous behavior. Scholars often donate their books they no longer use to a certain school in poor mountainous areas. Noted public figures often donate money for disaster relief. (3) _____, donation is a kind act, but it does not always make a generous man. We also frequently give our old possessions to those in need when we (4) _____ or are not attached to them any longer. It does not show that we are generous, though it is perhaps praiseworthy, as we (5) _____ and they could (6) _____ others, even though (7) _____.

As we often see, many famous entrepreneurs have donated to various charities for years on end. They have (8) _____ their philanthropy. Most people believe that what (9) _____ to do so is to boost their social recognition and publicity.

True generosity comes from heart rather than a strong sense of duty. (10) _____ _____ the wellbeing of others is part of his being a generous man. It seems that when (11) _____ helping others, he never misses. He seems to be eternally altruistic. Then (12) _____ his state of mind. His is an empathy state of mind. He knows by intuition what others really need and are ready to make his hours (13) _____ those around him and do whatever is good to those around him. And they do so, even without being aware of being generous.

II Now write an essay of about 220 words on *Generosity*. You may use the phrases from the box above.

Unit 8 **Generosity**

TEXT B Why We Should Always Be Kind to Strangers

Whitney Anthony

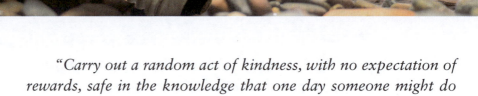

"Carry out a random act of kindness, with no expectation of rewards, safe in the knowledge that one day someone might do the same for you."—Princess Diana

Recently I was reminded of the importance of kindness, particularly kindness to strangers.

I was given the opportunity to film the wedding of a family friend. As a **videographer**, I'm always looking for ways to build my client base and enhance my professional experience, so naturally, I agreed.

Most of the guests at this wedding were friends of my parents, many of whom I hadn't seen in years. Although I recognized a lot of the people, most did not recognize me, particularly with a camera in my hand and "on the other side of the fence", so to speak.

A few kind souls were extremely friendly, looked me in the eyes, sparked conversation, and spoke to me with **dignity**. But to my surprise, the vast majority of guests at this wedding pushed past me, bumped into me, or spoke down to me. Again, these were people that I knew!

If we had been in any other situation—if perhaps, for example, my parents had been there with me—I'm certain these very same people would be giving me hugs and asking about my life with convincing interest.

But instead, I was treated as I was seen, like just another person in the service industry. It was as if an invisible fence existed between "us" and "them".

What bothered me most was not the poor treatment I received,

videographer *n.* 摄像师

dignity *n.* 尊严

but this notion of separateness that was so **pervasive** in the once familiar atmosphere around me. Here I was amongst families with whom I grew up, and those who did not recognize me treated me as though I was not worth recognizing. As if I wasn't even here.

While the looks I received symbolized separateness, what they provided for me was an **instantaneous** sense of wholeness.

Almost immediately, I'm reminded of the homeless man who holds a sign beside me as I wait for the **stoplight** to turn green and try to keep my eyes **averted**. Or the clerk at the McDonald's **drive-thru**, at whom I roll my eyes when I'm late for a meeting and she's slow to deliver my **vanilla** iced coffee.

In this moment, we are one. And that's when it hits me.

We're each a part of a whole, and everything we do (every thought, word, and deed) affects the whole. My mind **wanders** to the countless individuals who are **disregarded** in some way, shape, or form, every minute of every day.

We've all experienced it and we've all been a party to it.

Why do we do this to each other? What is this invisible fence dividing us vs. them? Where did it come from? And why is it **popping up** across all areas of our lives?

Safe in the **confines** of our car, we feel distant from those who stand on cold corners asking for our help. In our own **bubble** of a morning **ritual**, we forget that our coffee servers have morning rituals of their own. A false reality exists around us, and most often, without even giving it a second thought, we choose to live in it.

Like a prison built on the **delusional** foundation that we are somehow separate from one another, we're trapped. But what if we chose to live in truth instead? If we can recognize the intrinsic unity of humanity, perhaps we can finally be free.

Much like disregard, kindness for others is **cyclical** by nature. Kindness **begets** further kindness. And you never know how a simple "thank you" or smile could affect someone on any given day.

To be acknowledged and appreciated are among two of the greatest and most basic human needs. If we can **fulfill** this in one another with small acts of kindness that **perpetuate** themselves,

pervasive *adj.* 弥漫的，遍布的

instantaneous *adj.* 瞬间的

stoplight *n.* 交通信号灯
averted *adj.* 转移的
drive-thru *n.* 汽车餐厅
vanilla *n.* 香草

wander *vi.* 走神，开小差
disregard *vt.* 忽视

pop up 忽然出现
confine *n.* 边界
bubble *n.* 泡沫
ritual *n.* 惯例

delusional *adj.* 幻想的；错觉的

cyclical *adj.* 循环的
beget *vt.* 产生

fulfill *vt.* 实现
perpetuate *vt.* 使持续

why would we ever choose to do otherwise?

It's the simple, unexpected acts of generosity that change lives, and a culmination of these small acts can change the world.

Let's acknowledge the security guards and say "thank you" to the janitors. Let's start acting as if conversation we have is the most important one we will have all day. Let's look for the good in other people, and when we find it, let's treat them as though that's all we see.

We don't have to expect anything in return in order to be kind. With kindness, the giver benefits just as much, if not more, than the receiver.

Let's make it our goal to make at least one person's day, every day, and see how our own lives are transformed in the process. After all, we're all in this together…

culmination *n.* 结局

janitor *n.* 管理员，看护人

Notes

1. **Withney Anthony**

   Withney Anthony graduated from The University of North Carolina at Chapel Hill. She founded an inspirational website called Vehicle of Wisdom and a video production company, VOW Creative, LLC. She is the author of *10 Lies We Tell Ourselves* and *"Mother" as a Verb Rather than a Noun*.

2. **Princess Diana (Line 3)**

   Princess Diana (1961–1997) married Charles, Prince of Wales, on July 29, 1981. She is remembered as "People's Princess" for her widespread popularity and global humanitarian efforts.

3. **McDonald's drive-thru (Lines 37–38)**

   "McDonald's drive-thru" is the special name of McDonald's drive-thru restaurant. The first McDonald's drive-thru was built in 1975. The drive-through business model allows customers to complete their shopping in their cars through three windows. Customers order in the first window, pay in the second window, pick up the food in the third window, and drive away. All restaurants have a maximum stay time of three minutes from car entry to exit.

EXERCISES

A Reading for Gist

Answer the following questions according to your understanding of Text B.

1. Why should we always be kind to strangers according to the writer?

   _____

   _____

2. What can we learn from the writer's experience as a photographer?

   _____

   _____

B Reading for Details

Decide whether the following statements are true (T) or false (F).

1	I was invited to host the wedding of a family friend.	T F
2	Most of the guests at the wedding recognized me.	T F
3	What bothered me most at the wedding was the notion of separateness.	T F
4	When we sit in our car waiting for the light to turn green, we feel close to a homeless man who holds a sign asking for our help.	T F
5	Being cyclical, kindness for others produces further kindness.	T F
6	The accumulation of small generous acts can change the world.	T F

Unit 8 Generosity 233

C Reading Beyond

Discuss in small groups the difficulties of communicating with strangers on university campus and share the strategies on how to overcome them.

D Prefabs

Write the Chinese meanings of the following prefabs in the text.

safe in the knowledge that… _____

the vast majority of _____

What bothers me most is… _____

give it a second thought _____

basic human needs _____

so to speak _____

speak down to sb. _____

a sense of wholeness _____

by nature _____

in return _____

E Sentence Translation

I Translate the English sentences into Chinese.

1. Carry out a random act of kindness, with no expectation of rewards, safe in the knowledge that one day someone might do the same for you.

2. A false reality exists around us, and most often, without even giving it a second thought, we choose to live in it.

3. We're each a part of a whole, and everything we do (every thought, word, and deed) affects the whole.

II Translate the Chinese sentences into English, using the expressions in the brackets.

1. 那小狗可以说是家庭的一员了。(*so to speak*)

2. 如今歌坛新人辈出，却难见新人长久。(*pop up*)

3. 对这句话又想了一想之后，他明白了它的真正含义。(*give a second thought*)